Earl C. Kelley began his career in education in 1913 as a high school teacher. He was Dean of the Milwaukee Vocational School from 1929 to 1938, and in 1940 began educating high school teachers, subsequently helping to found the Youth Bureau of the Detroit Police Department and the Detroit Commission for Children and Youth. Today, Dr. Kelley is Professor of Secondary Education at Wayne State University. Among his published works are *Education for What Is Real* (1947), *The Workshop Way of Learning* (1951), and *Education and the Nature of Man* (1952) with Rasey.

IN DEFENSE OF YOUTH

IN DEFENSE OF YOUTH

Earl C. Kelley

PRENTICE-HALL, INC.
Englewood Cliffs, N.J.

To the memory of Howard Lane,

who understood our young and cared about them

Current printing (last digit):
14 13 12 11 10 9 8

Library of Congress Catalog Card Number: 62-13601
PRINTED IN THE UNITED STATES OF AMERICA 45919-C

Preface

I am not easily driven to my desk to write. I can always think of many more pleasant ways to spend my time. The circuitous route I take from the breakfast table to my desk reminds me of the way we used to approach a bumblebees' nest when I was a farm boy.

So I had to be pretty well steamed up to write even a short book. This condition came from the continuous assaults in our courts, our jails, through our mass media by adults on our own young. I was forced to the conclusion that adults do not really like their own young; that youth and age are in conflict; and adults always strike the first blow.

Many of us still seem to believe that there is nothing which violence will not cure. This is believed in spite of the overwhelming evidence that violence never really cured anything. Violence can only be inflicted by the stronger on the weaker. I am sure now of one thing: that if our young were born big and grew small, an entirely different set of individuals would get the beatings.

A citizen of Michigan recently made the proposal to the delegates of our Constitutional Convention that each community be required by the constitution to have a public whipping post. He specified that it be used to punish our "young punks" and for wife beaters. Of course the public whipping post is a splendid idea, but I want it used on motorists who blow their horns at me a split second before the traffic light turns green. Perhaps there is a little murder lurking in every heart.

The conflict between age and youth is such a sad state of affairs, and it is so contrary to my own experience with our young that it seemed a clear requirement that I at least put down on paper some of the things I have learned by association with young people. My experience does not square with what I have been reading, seeing and hearing. I wanted to do what I could to set the record straight.

Since I am a part of all that I have met, I am indebted to thousands for the ideas expressed here. Foremost on my list I want to mention the young people who attended the Milwaukee Vocational School during the depression years of 1929-38. These were the educationally disinherited from a large city. Their lives must have been bleak, since all were poor and many were on relief. They taught me that young people want a good society, and that adults do not have a corner on virtue. I want to mention especially those who were officers in the School Council, and those who were members of the Alumni Council, but of course their work would have been in vain if it had not been for the cooperation of those who were merely citizens of the school.

A good many of my colleagues helped me. Associate Dean J. W. Menge and Dr. Morrel J. Clute met with me evenings and gave careful criticism and suggestions. Dr. Roland C. Faunce went over the manuscript carefully and added many helpful ideas; so did Drs. George L. Miller and Theodore D. Rice. Professor Richard Brandt of the University of Maryland sent me much research material. Dr. Arthur Combs of the University of Florida did a thorough study of the first draft. My wife, Marne, and my daughter, Kate, not only did a good deal of the labor, but furnished criticism and encouragement as well.

E.C.K.

Table of Contents

Part I

It's hard to be young in these times

Chapter 1

Introduction

No species can survive on the earth unless it can invent ways by which its young can fully develop to maturity. Many species have disappeared because they did not succeed in doing this.

Most species, both plant and animal, do not nurture their young but depend upon enormous production of potential young and the chance that by so doing, at least one spore, seed, or egg will fall into circumstances enabling it to survive. A single puff ball, for example, produces billions of spores, literally filling the atmosphere with them. Yet it must be that on the average only one spore from each survives, since the earth's supply of puff balls does not seem to increase. The profligate production and ingenious methods of distributing seeds are well known.

Human beings, of course, cannot assure the reproduction of their kind in this manner. We produce our young in small number, and then they are not able to survive and develop without nurture. They are born with almost helpless bodies and with brains which have to be built through a long period of time. The meaning of the long infancy lies in the fact that the cortex of the brain has to be developed through a long period of social contact and can be developed in no other way. At birth full maturity is at least twenty years away. A certain amount of nurture from adult humans is required all of that time.

Lower animals—dogs and cats for example—require only a short period of nurture because their bodies grow to the adult stage rapidly and they do not have sizable cortices to develop in order to be adult.

Human parents have in the past been able to provide the needed nurture for their young. But in the recent past a profound change has taken place in the conditions under which our young grow up. We have become industrialized, and we have moved close together, depriving youth of many conditions under which it formerly thrived. This has happened nearly all over the world, and the problem of proper nurture of our young is a world-wide one.

The problem which we must face is whether we who live in cities can properly provide for the development of our young. We are not doing it now as every issue of every newspaper attests. Perhaps we cannot do it under these conditions. If this is true, we have already witnessed the beginning of the decline of the human race.

We have, of course, many reasons for hoping that the condition of youth shall be good. Youth are human beings and are entitled to all of the goods due to those who are human. Our own self-respect is at stake. Without good conditions for our young we will not have to wait until our youth take over in order to witness the collapse of our culture. Whenever we do things to diminish other human beings the harm is greater to ourselves than it is to the ones diminished. It is difficult to have a thriving human culture based on bad conscience. This is the reason, in part at least, why I think our attitudes toward youth are so important and so central.

We have no lack of pious words with regard to youth. It is a favorite topic with orators. Service clubs, for example, listen to these orations and applaud vigorously. And this oratory and its accompanying applause are sincere enough at the moment. But when we get away from the oratory, what we actually do speaks much more loudly than our applause. It is somewhat similar to what we do in church on Sunday. We hear about and agree with the concept of the brotherhood of man, but too often this feeling does not last until Monday. Throughout the week we forget the brotherhood of man, start working for our brother's disadvantage, renew our prejudices toward people unlike ourselves in race or religion, become bad or indifferent neighbors, show small concern for the disparity in human circumstance among our brothers.

I am concerned about the condition of children as well as youth. Many babies are so damaged that they cannot avoid unhappy and difficult times when they grow into youth. But here I shall deal only with the problems of youth, because improving the lot of little children is an important and separate task. Our attention is most often upon youth, perhaps because they are bigger, more mobile, and more likely to disturb the lives of all who live in the community. Youth are, I believe, less understood, and more subject to adult aggression, less heir to the benefits of love and the milk of human kindness than are babies and young children.

Chapter 2

Many Hold False Ideas About Youth

I have wanted to say that the general public does not understand youth, but this is too mild. Not only do we not understand them, we hold false notions about them. These ideas do not result merely in our being puzzled about young people; they cause us to take action in the wrong direction. These ideas and their results have not only been disproved by research but have failed us again and again through the ages. To cling to them is to fall back far beyond the age of science and reason to the pre-scientific days of witchcraft and even back to voodooism. Some of these false ideas are listed below.

1) *Many believe that children are born bad and have to be coerced into being good.* This accounts for many acts of aggression committed by adults on babies even in the cradle. These acts are sometimes perpetrated on infants so young that they have not yet even gained their eyesight or their sense of hearing. What such an infant can feel about this is that he has been born into a hostile world. The idea that children are born bad accounts for the "training" concept which rightly belongs to the rearing of animals, such as horses and dogs, but is never successful with humans. This is the opposite of the concept of growth and education. While training seeks to close the mind so that only one response will be available, education in its true sense is designed to open the mind, to reveal the wide world, and to make an infinite number of responses possible. Modern science has shown that children are born neither good nor bad. "Goodness" and "badness" are adult concepts, and they are learned. They are products of the lives people lead from birth on. They depend upon the quality of living available to the young over which the young have no control.

2) *Many believe that youth has gone to the dogs.* This is an idea which seems to be firmly implanted in the minds of most adults. One is tempted to attribute it to the changed conditions under which we live. But when we realize that this complaint is in the literature almost as far back as written language goes, we see that we would still have this complaint

even if we had not changed the conditions under which we live. The citation of these complaints could fill a large book and would become extremely tiresome. Perhaps it will suffice to quote Socrates, who lived four hundred years before Christ, and to add that this sentiment has been repeated *ad nauseam* ever since, reaching new depths in the last year or two. Twenty five hundred years ago Socrates is quoted as having said:

> Children now love luxury. They have bad manners, contempt for authority. They show disrespect for elders, and love chatter in place of exercise. Children are now tyrants, not the servants of their households.

It seems odd, but the very people who complain about modern youth often like to tell in glowing terms of their own depredations when they were boys. Of course, a story is always improved in the telling, but even after discounting for this, some of the reminiscent confessions are amply horrifying. It is true that more of the shortcomings of youth come to our attention because we live closer together than we did formerly, because we have invented probation officers and juvenile courts, and because people dearly love to read about delinquency. Since we live closer together and there are more of us, there is doubtless more anti-social behavior among some young people.

The over-all evidence, however, is that youth as a whole behave better than they ever did. Careful research has shown that they read better, spell better, and cipher better than they ever did. Not only that, but school discipline and behavior are better than ever before. It is now unheard of for a school to be closed because the students are out of control. But in 1837, one hundred and fifty schools in Massachusetts alone were closed for this reason. In Boston in 1850, it took sixty-five beatings a day to keep a school of four hundred going. About 1875, an uncle of mine decided on teaching as a career and started with a country one-room school. His professional career ended when the pupils tipped the outhouse over, door down, with him in it. I never heard how he got out, but by the time I knew him he was an aging farmer.

Indeed, in my time, the idea that the function of the pupils was to throw out the teacher was not yet dead. The first teaching I did was in a one-room, eight-grade country school where my predecessor had been vanquished. It was a peculiar school in that, though public, it had only boys in it. I learned that nobody would send a girl to the school because it was considered too tough. I have always wondered about it because, although I was only eighteen years old and weighed less than 130 pounds dripping wet (I went into teaching instead of farming because I wasn't very good at farm work) nobody bothered me at all. No pupil ever laid a hand on me, or I on him. The only brush with destiny I had was when one of the fathers came in after school when I was alone and told me that he was going to "thrash me within an inch of my life." This seemed odd, because I thought I was getting along fine with his boy. Since he had stated his errand, however, I picked up the stove poker and said that then was the best time to try. He retreated through the open door, and I never saw him again.

I tell this to make the point that the only trouble I had was with an adult and that I cannot conceive how the former teacher got himself ejected unless he subjected these pupils to extreme aggravation. My success must have come from what I did not do rather than what I did. I did not know any child psychology and my confidence was only exceeded by my ignorance.

Youth, it seems to me, have been getting better instead of worse in spite of living under more difficult circumstances than was formerly the case.

3) *It is often said that parents do not love their young these days.* Many people believe that parents have become irresponsible and that they no longer care what happens to their young. If parents really cared about their young, they would see to it that their youth did not bother you and me as they now do.

It is true, of course, that some parents care more than others. This has, however, probably always been the case, since people are unique in every way. In the farm community where I grew up, before the automobile had become a factor in our lives, there were parents who seemed to take less care of their young than others. I expect this will always be true.

But in all studies of the nature of the human organism, or of the animals less than human, there is nothing to indicate that parental love has lessened. Parental love for the young is deep-seated and persistent. It can be observed in many of the lower animals. It has had survival value throughout the long history of mankind. How this powerful force, working through the ages, could lessen or disappear in one generation is impossible to explain.

Parents do have to rear their young under more difficult circumstances than they did before America became so heavily industrialized. I shall have more to say about this shortly. There is no reason to believe that they care less; on the contrary, because it is more difficult, they probably are more concerned than ever before. On account of these difficulties they are entitled to our sympathy and understanding, rather than our blame and scorn.

4) *Many believe that violence will cure any youth of anything.* The same people who believe that parents no longer care about their young accuse them of being over-indulgent. This must mean that parents love their children too much. These people often aver that there is nothing the matter with our youth that a good licking wouldn't cure. They want parents to substitute the knout for love. This belief in the value of violence is so common in our culture that it is frightening. It would seem that the evils of violence would be so apparent, after milleniums of its use, that we would at last be ready to at least try something else. These words may never be finished because we, through our age-long pursuit of violence as a cure for everything, may render this beautiful earth a dead planet, not only devoid of human life but also of blameless, peace-loving animals and the plants on which they depend. Yet many still cry "Hit him!" "Beat him!" "Jail him!"

These people get their impulses from far in the past, in the pre-scientific days when man was far more naïve than he is now supposed to be. These impulses or beliefs come from the days of the iron maiden and the whipping post. Those were the days when elderly helpless women were thrown into a river. If they floated, they were witches and were taken out, dried off, and burned. If they sank, they were not witches and died an honorable, though watery, death. In those days, the mentally ill were often beaten to drive out the evil spirits.

Although the return of the whipping post is often advocated in the public press (not editorially, so far as I know), the laws of our nation have gradually become more enlightened. Our jails are often degrading and our chain gangs are utterly inhuman, but we no longer beat people in public, and many states in the Union have accepted the futility of capital punishment as a control over behavior.

It seems to me that the biggest lesson the human race could learn, while it can still learn, is that violence never gained anything in the long history of man. "A good beating" never made youth better, even though it might appear to have done so. It never served any purpose except to make youth more fearful, more hostile, more secretive, and more aggressive. It never drew parent and child closer together, but always pushed them farther apart. I would go so far as to say that, unless the youth has been too badly damaged, there is nothing a good loving will not cure. This, of course, applies to our relationships with each other as well as with youth, and if it could spread all over the world, it would be the way to peace. We cannot be at war with our youth and at peace with those more remote from us.

Chapter 3

We Don't Like Youth Very Well

I have come to this conclusion reluctantly. As previously noted, our literature during the last 2400 years at least reveals this fact. Today's magazines and newspapers probably devote as much space to this topic as to the bomb and our threatening doom. Our youth, when they are talking about their elders among themselves, reveal it. The wrangling that goes on in many homes attests to this fact. The conflict between age and youth is one of the saddest aspects of our culture. And the saddest fact of all is that age always strikes the first blow.

I am aware that many adults do love youth. Earlier I referred to the oratory at the service clubs. The speakers and the listeners are both sincere, at least at the moment. Some forget their noble sentiments when they go back to getting and spending; others do not. I have known men and women who cared so much about the welfare of youth that they gave all of their time and spent much of their money for youth's betterment.

It is the manner in which our society as a whole—our parents, our teachers, our government, our citizens—behaves regarding youth that we have to examine here. The good people cited above are not enough. No one person, no hundred persons, can do enough on this huge problem to accomplish more than to set an example. We who want our democracy to survive have to see where our values lie and have to learn to give not only our money, but our attitudes and our love. Hostile attitudes on the part of the elders are quickly sensed by youth whose response in many instances is hostility and aggression.

We Provide Poorly for Them

A good measure, however, of our attitudes toward youth may be gained by the money we are willing to spend for them. The young have many needs, but a good place to start would be to provide them with good schools taught by well-educated, competent, well-paid teachers. This would not answer all of youth's needs, but it would be a good beginning. On the whole, however, we seem to be unwilling to do even this much. I do not know, except by inference, how the schools are faring in other parts of the country, but in Michigan we are in a continuous uproar about getting the voters to approve taxes for our schools. Many of the proposals turned down by the voters are most niggardly to begin with. In many cities of this state schools are being operated on half-time schedules. Parts of the curriculum enjoyed by youth are being cut out, leaving only the parts young people dislike. The building of new schools is being discontinued. Old buildings are being left to deteriorate. One community has two new buildings already finished which are standing idle because there is no staff for them. All this goes on at the very time when the burgeoning crop of postwar babies is coming to school, and the trend is toward larger and larger families.

This is also the time when we have never before been so wealthy. It will not serve any good purpose here for me to quote statistics on annual income and related evidences of wealth. I think no one will question the fact that the United States today has more wealth and a higher standard of living than any large country has ever had at any time in the history of mankind. Yet it is not uncommon to read in the public press that we simply cannot carry the tax load needed to support good schools.

Sidney Harris, whose daily column is filled with intelligent comment on the current scene and whose writings I recommend most highly to any who may read these words, treats of our penury in regard to the support of education (April 1, 1959; Detroit *Free Press*). He says in brief that we are schizophrenic in this matter. We all believe in good schools but seem also to believe in magic and think that if we go to enough PTA meetings, or find enough fault, or pick on our youth enough, our schools will become magnificent institutions by magic and without cost.

He goes on to say that we do not apply magic to our businesses or any of our many other enterprises; that we know these take money, effort, planning, and a goal. He calls attention to the fact that when many children die in a school fire, as happened in Chicago recently, we pass resolutions forbidding the use of fire traps but provide nothing to eliminate them. This, Mr. Harris says, is schizophrenia. Such a society, I say, does not let the right hand know that the left hand is not doing anything. Anybody who wants to verify the above should read the minutes of the Detroit Common Council shortly after the Chicago school fire.

When the great depression of 1929 struck us, the first thing we did was to cut many facilities for youth. Schools needed then to be greatly expanded with much broadening of their offerings. This is obvious because there were so many youth who had no place else to go. But we cut school budgets severely, reduced the salaries of our teachers below what anybody could survive on, and took out all parts of the curriculum which might appeal to idle and disinherited youth. All other agencies for youth suffered similarly. Organized recreation, for example, was eliminated or greatly reduced. Idleness became the unwilling lot of our young. Despair followed closely. Some of our youth sat at home, some went out onto our streets and found release from boredom in anti-social behavior, some took to the road. There was a time, so it is said, when there were a million and a half boy and girl tramps on the highways of the richest country on earth. These young people became known as the lost generation. Why were they lost, and what was the cost?

They were lost because we cared more about our money than we did about our young. Of course, these were hard times for all of us. They were much harder than they needed to be, as we can see now. We thought we were financially ruined. It was said that our national debt was twenty billions and could not stand to be raised. If it was raised, the national credit would be gone. The last I heard, our federal debt now is 289 billions, and Uncle Sam's credit is still good. Most of this increase came during World War II. We found that to save our own hides we could get money. In 1933, perhaps our blackest year, we still had our beautiful land, our farms, our factories, and our houses. We simply did not know how to use them. So we saved on the most helpless in our society.

There is a large segment of the lost generation which we usually forget to count. It is the large number who never got started because our economic system prevented their being born. The number of unborn during the thirties must be in the millions. How many scientists, how many teachers, artists, musicians did we lose? We note that tax experts are aghast at the present birth rate. Do they want to wish away human beings with all of their unique potentialities? The only real value in this world is human beings, not forests, oil wells or mines. It is humans which give all of those things value. Each human being that might have been born and was not represents an irreplaceable loss.

The lost generation were not, of course, all lost. Many were damaged needlessly, and some were indeed lost, in that they became criminals as a product of the lives we required them to live. Some became insane. Some were rescued by the creation of two federal agencies, the Civilian Conservation Corps (C.C.C.) and the National Youth Administration

(N.Y.A.). Some were just too resilient to be ruined. It takes a lot of doing to spoil a boy or girl. This is a good thing for us older ones. For this lost generation was the one which heroically threw itself in front of the oncoming war machine of the Nazi.

Those who survived this ordeal—and hundreds of thousands of them did not—are now in the early stages of middle age, heads of families, holding responsible positions in our society, reproducing like mad, and causing all kinds of future trouble for the taxpayers who think we are too poor to care for our own.

I have dwelt on the plight of the schools partly, I suppose, because I am a teacher, and educational problems are closer to me than are some others. It also seems to me that for the citizen who is not schizophrenic, paying taxes for schools would be the easiest thing he could do for youth. This is the way he would get most for his money and effort. It would be much cheaper and easier than opening and supporting a teen canteen, for example, and would do more for youth if we really care about them.

Our record in providing other institutions is even more deplorable. Unfortunately, some of our youth, for the safety of the community and for themselves, have to be isolated and secured. Until quite recently we thought nothing of throwing them in jail or penitentiary with older, hardened criminals to absorb all of the fine points of crime and to learn all kinds of depravity. Some time in the early part of this century we saw that this was a harmful way to treat children. We built detention homes, and our state penitentiaries for youth were called schools. In most states youth under a certain age could not be charged with a crime but could only be judged to be delinquent.

This was a big step in the direction of more humane treatment of a segment of our youth. Of course, now when a boy is especially sick and commits a particularly violent act, there is a great cry that he must be "bound over" from the juvenile court to the criminal court where we can do a better job of "getting even" with him for what he has done. In other words we say "This boy is too sick for the best treatment we know about. Because he is so sick, we must give him our worst medicine."

Having established special institutions for youth, we have then failed to support them. Because of our parsimony these detention homes and state "schools," overcrowded and inadequately staffed, have had to become more and more like jails. We still dump dependent children, who are guilty of nothing but having no one to take care of them, into these "homes."

For the past five or ten years a great hullabaloo has been heard in the state of Michigan over the location of a new state school for boys. For many years the so-called "Vocational School" for boys, in Lansing, was outdated, overcrowded and inadequate. What is perhaps even worse, it occupied considerable space right in the city—space that would be very valuable if it were sub-divided. The legislature had finally appropriated funds—no small achievement if you know our legislature—to build a new school out somewhere where there will be more space and property will be cheaper. But whenever a site was chosen, lawsuits and injunctions were brought by citizens who lived near the site and who thought some other part of the state would be better. It appeared that we would never get the new school because nobody wanted it in the same county with him. We had a few bleak and desolate spots in the northern part of our otherwise beautiful state, far from friends and relatives, and it appeared that one of those places, where there were only pine stumps to protest, would have to be used for our new boys' school. We did, however, finally get a good location for the new school.

It will not profit us, I think, to pursue further this story of adult neglect of the needs of youth. The failure to provide adequately for the brain-injured, the spastics, the mentally ill would only labor the point. "Oh masters, if I were disposed to stir your hearts and minds with mutiny and rage . . ."

We use our youth as scapegoats. Often when we ourselves fail, we blame it on our young. This is not new, but recent events point to this fact dramatically.

When Russia launched her first satellite in October, 1957, it not only scared the living daylights out of us, but hurt our pride almost beyond repair. Up to that time we had assumed that we could do everything better than anybody else anywhere. And when our armed forces began to shoot those Roman candles which fell at their feet on Cape Canaveral in an absurd effort to show that we are as smart as anybody else, we almost died of humiliation.

When we looked around for someone to blame, we did not see the Pentagon, large as it is. We did not see the Congress, which appropriates funds for such matters. We did not see the Commander-in-Chief who, within the limits of what Congress provides, controls such matters. Whom did we see? We saw our youth! Here was the perfect scapegoat—perfect because youth has little power to strike back. The logic is clear. (Logic is often a way to get the wrong answer in an orderly fashion.) We did not beat Russia because we have inferior scientists. This is true because our youth are lazy, indolent, fun-loving, and will not study "hard" subjects. This in spite of the fact that the scientists who were working on our missiles were educated in "the good old days," which are never further back than the childhood of the complainers.

I am still enough of a hundred percent red-blooded American to think that we could have launched the first satellite if we had been willing to make the sacrifice and had not starved or hounded some of our best scientists out of government service.

Then began the most vicious vilification of our youth that has ever occurred in our history. This never could have happened before, because we did not have the mass media previously. Nearly every newspaper, magazine, radio and television station took up the hue and cry. Facts and truth were quite forgotten and ignored. In attacking youth it was logical to include their teachers, who also were relatively helpless and who were, of course, partly to blame for youth's shiftlessness which bordered on treason. A sad aspect of it was that many teachers were stupid enough and masochistic enough to join the pack. It was scapegoating at its worst.

As a result of this reaction to fear and hurt pride, we now find our youth under pressure as never before. And this at a time in their growth when they ought to be expanding into life. This pressure is particularly severe if a youth is so unfortunate as to be considered "gifted." He has had his homework doubled, and some otherwise sane people recommend as much as six hours a night. He has had his grades reduced, despite the fact that he is doing more work than ever. This is the way teachers show that they do too have high standards. I believe that at this particular time our so-called gifted youth are more discriminated against than any other group.

How much leisure does the adult who thinks six hours of homework is about right demand for himself? Even though he may not know any better than to overwork, he hardly would commit himself to that much work after hours. But it's good for growing youth!

To be sure our youth are a good deal more intelligent than we give them credit for, and many have found that the best thing to do is to fail tests so they will not be chosen for special punishment. It is the medium smart who are really catching it.

We use our youth as means to our own ends. This is what is going on with the present demand that every child shall be a scientist and a mathematician. There has been no outcry from youth for this. It is entirely because adults are frightened and think that if the whole population were making missiles, they would somehow be safe. As is always the case, when anyone sticks his nose into business he does not understand, he runs the chance of looking silly.

When we got into World War II we dearly loved the youth we had neglected. Nothing was too good for our boys as long as they went out and fought our battles. Even the colleges, which found themselves nearly devoid of students, found that they could take some who would previously have been rejected. Welcome signs hung from every elm on the campus, and almost any 4F whose body was warm could get in. That was because adults work in colleges, and while students are an awful nuisance to some of them, they still must have a student body.

Terrible things portend for the next war, if it comes, but next time youth will not be in any more jeopardy than anyone else. Indeed, the armed services may be the safest place to be.

Thus I am forced to the sad conclusion that we do not like youth very well. If we did, we would not quarrel with them so much. We would not use them as scapegoats. We would not use them as means to our own ends. We would be more willing to spend our riches on them. We would learn better how to live with them.

Chapter 4

The New Problems of Youth

Cities Are Made for Adults

We have for the most part become an urban nation. This has happened very rapidly. In my lifetime I have observed most of this change. This seems to be a long time to me and probably to you, but it is a mere flicker of time in the long history of mankind. The change from rural to urban living was inevitable, made so by the creation of new means of energy outside our own bodies. When I was born we had virtually no energy except that of our own bodies and of our domesticated animals. The steam engine had been invented, which affected us on the farm very little. The internal combustion engine also had been invented but had not yet been put to use in such ways as transportation. The automobile was yet to come. We got water out of the well by the use of wind, but that was about all the help we had and the wind did not always blow. Then we had to pump water for the stock, and twenty head of cattle can drink a great deal on a hot, still evening.

I do not want to appear to contend that we all should have stayed on the farm, or that we should return to it. That was a hard, lonely life, and the rewards were few. Life ought to be infinitely better in our industrialized, urbanized society, and it is, when we know how to take advantage of it.

We are not ourselves yet adjusted to urban life so that we can happily and contentedly take advantage of it. This needs to be pointed out because, when we take a blameful attitude toward youth, we must realize that it is much more difficult to grow up in 1960 than it was in 1910.

For one thing, the closer we live together the more we get in each other's hair—the more we need cooperation, patience, and human understanding. While farm living seemed to render us more patient, city living seems often to cause us to be more irritable, just at the time when we have more people around to irritate us.

In 1910 my brothers and I had 160 acres all to ourselves. We had the whole countryside besides, if we wanted it, for there were no "No Trespassing" signs. There were no houses where children were not welcome. To be sure, we were benighted in our attitudes toward people of races and religions different from ours. Nobody lived there anyway except our own kind, whom we believed to be God's anointed. But children and youth were not treated as an unwanted minority group.

We had real work to do, not made work. It was not necessary to argue with us about assuming responsibility. It was altogether apparent that the work had to be done if we wanted to eat. Nobody was thinking it up for us because he thought it would be good for us. There was so much hard work, all of which was necessary, that when it was done we had little energy left for "cussedness," though we had some to use that way. When we did behave in a way that would now be considered delinquent, there were no police or probation officers to worry about it, hardly any neighbors to complain, or any official to complain to. We had a sheriff in the county and a constable in the township, and they would have arrested us if we committed murder or robbery. Our minor depredations, however, rarely bothered anyone other than our own folks who would be unlikely to call on the law.

It was a hard life and a lonely one, but it had some extremely important advantages for youth not easily achieved in an urban situation. It had honest responsibility and necessary physical work which did not have to be "sold" to them. It had space where a boy could really expand without damaging anyone. It was free from most of the exclusions so well known to our urban youth.

Though urbanization was inevitable and ought to be desirable, we must not forget that we have, in the process, deprived our youth of many good things, most of which we have made no effort to replace, or do not know how to replace. If we take my city home as the center and consider the 160 acres surrounding it, there must be hundreds of children and youth living on it. On this "farm" are many lawns, many flower beds, much concrete paving, and many "Keep Off" signs.

It is very difficult to raise four boys on a forty-foot lot, as someone I know is trying to do. There is not much honest work for them to do. When they are at home with nothing to do, conflict between them and their elders is hard to avoid. And in comparison this is quite a privileged situation compared to other urbanized families. In any of our large cities families of this size can be found living in one room without benefit of modern heating, lighting or toilet facilities. When we start to criticize parents and their children, as we so often do, we need to ask ourselves how good parents we would be under these conditions. If parental love and responsibility have declined (which I do not believe), we must admit that many parents have had to operate under severe stress.

Laws Confine Youth

People often ask "Why doesn't that big lug of a boy next door quit school and go to work? He'll never learn anything anyway." This presents two other major ways in which we have changed the lot of youth. In 1910 this would have been easy to do. Anybody could quit school any time, and since we were all in a fight for mere survival, there was always plenty of work for him to do. We now have and need (1) compulsory school attendance laws and (2) child labor laws.

Compulsory school-attendance laws are necessary and justifiable in a democratic industrial society, because we cannot operate a close-knit democratic society without a literate electorate. We have every right to require that the first part of every citizen's life be devoted to formal education. It is central to the American dream that each person shall have an opportunity for self-improvement, and that there shall be no limit to what a person may achieve except his own limitations. This is one of the big ideas that is different in America from most of the rest of the world. Here one is not born into a "class" or a "station in life" in which he must live and die. Although this dream is imperfectly implemented, as our shameful behavior over integration attests, still it is the American ideal, partly realized. This is what gives the American hope, so essential to the release of human energy, and so lacking in some of the other countries.*

The public school is America's instrument for approaching equality of opportunity for all. It is probably the greatest social invention in the history of mankind. It is the fountain of hope for those born to despair. If we did not have it, we would indeed be hard put to come by it. We have every right to require all of our young citizens to be in attendance. Many of the problems of our schools came about because after about 1920 we adopted the concept of education for all. This is something which has come into our lives altering the conditions under which youth grow up. It is one answer to the question as to why the "big lug" does not quit school and get a job.

* Hadley Cantril, *The Politics of Despair* (N. Y.: Basic Books, Inc., 1958).

Child Labor Laws

One other powerful reason is that in most states we have enacted child labor laws which restrict youth employment. These laws were passed in part for humanitarian reasons. The history of early America with regard to the exploitation of children is not a pretty one. The story of young children spending twelve to fifteen hours a day in sweat shops is well known. There has been a natural revulsion against these practices, and now a good many states, though not all, prohibit them. It has not been possible, however, to get a prohibition of the abuses of children into our national constitution, that great document which so admirably proclaims and protects the rights of adults. For the past thirty or more years, there has been an amendment before the people which prohibits in a minimal way the exploitation of children. It has been passed by the two-thirds vote of Congress and signed by the President. But it has not received the approval of the required number of states.

If any one is interested, this amendment is known as the Child Labor Amendment. It has no number since nobody knows how many other amendments will be passed before this one is approved. It is still before the people, and can be approved at any time. In case one might think that it is only the rural southern states which have blocked the adoption, it might be worth noting that one state which has not passed the amendment is Michigan. Some people say that the Michigan legislature is fearful that the amendment might interfere with the farmer's right to exploit children. This seems likely to be the case, since our legislature has not hesitated to pass a good many laws restricting child and youth employment in industry.

At any rate many people become staunch supporters of "states' rights" when it comes to the exploitation and abuse of our young. It seems that what we do to our children is our own affair. These are often the same people who like to have the federal government butt into our affairs when it comes to building roads or harbors or dams or regulating labor. Some of them are asking the federal government to interfere in the management of youth, provided they do it in the right way. There is now considerable clamor for the revival of the Civilian Conservation Corps. Whatever the virtues of this corps, and there were a good many especially suited to the time when it thrived, it had one supreme virtue. That was that it took our youth hundreds of miles away where they could not bother us. The C.C.C. is a very expensive program, but then we're rich, aren't we? And besides, that is not real money, only federal money, so it actually won't cost us anything. All of that peace for free!

There Are Not Enough Jobs for All

One motive, then, for child labor laws was humanitarian. In a good many states the sight of children in sweat shops is a thing of the past. There is another motive which may be socially sound, if not so humanitarian. That is the job squeeze. Because of our lack of imagination there is a scarcity of employment at the very time that there is also a scarcity of goods. Let us not even mention the hundreds of millions of people, many of them children, in other parts of the world who have never known how it feels not to be hungry.

We have and have for a long time had a scarcity of jobs. This has been true, as I remember it, ever since about 1910, except in time of war. Even the cold war (1946—millennium) on which our present economy is so dependent has not kept us busy. This has meant that somebody gets squeezed. Who is the least able to resist a squeeze? Our youth, of course.

And so it comes about that in Michigan, while we do not approve the Child Labor Amendment, we prohibit anyone from getting a decent job before he is eighteen years old. Many kinds of employment are closed to youth until they are twenty-one. The penalties on business and industry for employing under-age youth are severe, especially if the illegally employed person happens to be injured. These laws fall most heavily on urban youth who have the most time on their hands.

I do not want it to appear that I think these youth labor laws are bad, particularly if we continue to believe in scarcity of employment. I doubt that it would be socially desirable for a sixteen-year-old boy to replace a thirty-five-year-old man with a family to house, clothe and feed. I believe, too, that we have a right to require that the first twenty-one years of each citizen's life be spent in education. That is, I believe this if we are prepared to furnish meaningful education to all, which we presently are not. I am merely explaining why, the social scene being what it is, that "big lug" next door does not go out and get a job.

In most states, including Michigan, compulsory school attendance ends at sixteen years of age. Youths leave school at sixteen in great hordes. They cannot get real employment until they are eighteen or more. At one time I estimated that in Detroit alone there were 50,000 young people who had left school, were virtually unemployed, and who were for the most part unknown to any school or any agency. This is not a reliable estimate, but it really does not matter. There are far too many. They are idling away their time in the urban situation, often in slum areas, where opportunities of constructive activity are almost nonexistent and where chances for mischief abound. There are many cars to steal, for example; it is easy to get a car when an adult has conveniently left the keys.

Of course, many of these idle young people have good homes located near recreational facilities. Even they have a hard time passing the days and nights legally and profitably, but thousands are not so fortunate. This is a big segment of our society concerning which we never hear unless trouble arises.

For the past few pages I have sought to show that our young people are not an inferior lot, as so many seem to think. There is no reason in scientific thinking to account for any such change. We are not planting inferior seed, but we have changed the conditions under which our young are nurtured. In many ways we have improved their lot, but we have deprived them of some extremely important things for which we have as yet provided no substitute. We have made them look worse than they used to. Indeed, in some instances we have made them behave worse.

Chapter 5

Some Become Delinquent

The last sentence in the preceding chapter brings me to one of the favorite discussion topics of the adult world. Many of us seem to be morbidly enchanted with the whole topic of sin. When the sins are committed by one of our scapegoat minorities, we seem to relish them all the more. Many pages of our newspapers and magazines are devoted to this topic. Many self-anointed experts expound the topics. Then there are a good many hard-working scientists who have devoted years to research in juvenile delinquency. They have given us a great deal more to go on in meeting the problem than we formerly had. They have been more interested in why certain youth are delinquent than they are in what the depredations were or how many were involved. We all owe a great deal to these researchers, and we consult them too little when we want to make a speech or write an article.

Of course, we do have considerable anti-social behavior on the part of youth in our modern urban society. Some of these youths commit serious crimes, and some are extremely dangerous. They do a great deal of damage, and their cost in money alone is enormous. The cost of that part of the police force taken up by juveniles, the cost of courts and their probation and parole officers, the cost of jailing or detention, must run to billions a year. This is not to mention the human costs. How do we measure the value of people injured or killed by youth crime, or the sorrow and guilt of the parents of the offenders? How do we figure the cost of losing the offenders from productive activity?

And while we are discussing the losses due to delinquency, let us not forget what it costs us for failing to develop the potentialities of the youth who are not delinquent. How can we afford to have millions of youth who, for economic reasons, cannot obtain educational opportunities? How can we afford a minority group whose capacities seldom get a chance to become useful? In the Negro people alone, not to mention other minorities, we lose enormous quantities of possible talent through bigotry and fear.

Juvenile delinquency appears to be a modern city problem for the most part. It is to a considerable degree an automobile problem. In many cases it involves cars in one way or another. Sometimes the car is stolen, or there is speeding or reckless driving. Acts of delinquency are usually not committed at home, or even within walking distance of home.

To be sure youth has always engaged in some anti-social behavior. We do not know how much, partly because in our rural living we did not separate the "criminals" on the basis of age as we do now. The jail, the whipping post, and the gallows were for young and old alike. Then, too, there must have been a great deal of socially unacceptable behavior that went undetected. Any of my contemporaries can recall, I am sure, acts of his youth for which he probably would have been arrested if there had been anyone around to do the arresting. We must not let our logic lead us to decide that police and probation officers are what cause delinquency. Groucho Marx said, many years ago when he was playing the part of an employer in one of his comedies, "What makes wage slaves? Wages make wage slaves, so let's do away with wages."

Probation officers, police and judges do not cause delinquency, but they do cause statistics. Since we did not have them in the "good old days," we do not have statistics for that time. It is altogether evident, however, that we do have many more behavior problems with our young than we used to have. This comes primarily, as has been said, not because we have an inferior biological crop, but because we have put too many of them to the acre, with too little to do.

Not only is it impossible to make accurate comparisons of delinquency between the present and the past, but we do not know how much we have right now. We know it is too much, because any delinquency is too much. But each community has its own way of figuring. One community doubled its delinquency overnight statistically, although the youth were behaving the same. This was done merely by changing the rule as to what should be counted as delinquent. Statistics on delinquency are quite unreliable.

There are two general types of juvenile delinquents. We cannot say that each belongs to one type or the other. But if we look at the extremes, we can see them better.

Some Are Victims of Circumstance

The first is the boy (girls are not so likely to fall into this class) who is a perfectly normal young human being who gets into trouble because he is full of animal spirit and is living without enough space to burn it up constructively. He may be an excellent student and a leader in his school life. He goes out with his peers to have some fun, and one thing leads to another. He becomes more daring than he normally would be, and consequences seem remote. He may carry this to the point where he violates the law in some way. It may be in a small way, or it may be something serious. An automobile may be involved somehow. Somebody may get injured. The first thing he knows, he has been arrested and charged with a crime when all he meant to do was to have fun and companionship. He and all like him are in a sense victims of circumstance.

True, this boy should not have done it, or so it seems to his elders who no longer can even feel the spirit that impelled him. We are right in trying to keep such behavior to a minimum. We need to remember, however, that young people's bodies grow faster than their judgment, and youth are men in stature and are able to burst their city-imposed bounds before they can think about social consequences.

It must be said that society makes some effort to protect this type of delinquent. If he is under seventeen, he is not charged with a crime, and often police and judges try to keep his arrest off the records. But often this is not so. Society levels the full weight of its blame upon him. His parents often act as though they had been personally affronted and that the boy had done what he did "to drag their proud name through the mud." The boy has probably heard his father brag about what he did in the good old days and sigh because boys aren't boys any more.

For this type of youth, being arrested may have far more serious consequences than the act or the intent warrants. A common question on recommendation blanks, especially for military or other governmental service is, "Have you ever been arrested on a criminal charge?" The implication is that if he has, he will not be accepted. I suppose there is hardly anyone in our modern society who has never been arrested, if only for making an illegal left turn. It leads one to wonder how far our military and governmental services fare if they are made up only of people who never tested the bonds of modern living.

The consequences of what would formerly have been normal mischief are much greater than they used to be. The scorn is greater. While it is important that this boy understand that his act must not be repeated, most of all we must make him realize that we love him and have confidence in him. The feeling that every finger is pointed at him, not on his account but because he has shamed his school or church, or parents—that it is *their* pride that really matters—cannot help. Rejection is quite likely to lead to deliberate rebellion, which was not intended at all in the beginning.

Some Youth Are Damaged

The second type of delinquent is much more serious than the first. Again we can see these two types best by looking at the extremes. There are a good many cases of delinquency which are not clearly one type or the other. The second type are the damaged, the unwanted, the unassimilated, the unloved. In many cases they have been born into the world unwanted and in poverty. They are the product of the lives they have lived, as indeed everybody is. They are psychological cripples, and they cannot live normal lives. It is the psychological structure which determines how one will function—what he will do. We all need good bodies, to be sure, and some of these psychological cripples have splendid physical structures. But the physical structure does not determine what a person will do; indeed it has little or nothing to do with behavior. One can be a saint or a sinner, a valedictorian or a pickpocket, with the same body. It is attitude, outlook, habit, cultural mores, which determine behavior.

We take pretty good care of our physical cripples. We are all attentive and respectful when a man with a white cane goes along the sidewalk. We treat polio victims in their wheel chairs with great deference. This is as it should be. We would behave differently toward the psychologically crippled if his condition was as plain as that of a paralytic. Our hearts would go out to him, because we could see that he had been stunted and warped since infancy. Pursuing this thought, however, I am afraid this would not be a very comfortable place to live if *all* of our own psychological selves were laid bare for all to see. Not that the psychological self and the physical self constitute a duality; they operate together as an entity, but there is no harm in speaking of them separately just as we speak of hand and foot. These are parts of a totality, functioning together. But the psychological self controls behavior, and when a big strong body has crippled controls, anti-social behavior is almost certain to result. This is the situation with most of our juvenile delinquents.

If most delinquency is the result of the crippling of the psychological self, how does this damage come about? Every one of us is what he is as a result of the life he has led. When a person has a damaged self the damage is usually done in his early years. Children who come through their early years with relatively little damage to the growth of personality rarely become delinquent except as might happen to anyone as described in the first type. A child cannot choose the quality of living available to him. If he is crippled, it has been done by adults over whom he has no control. This is done largely by withholding love, or giving love for the adult's goal rather than that of the child. Many times this is done one way or the other with the best of intentions. Some of us cannot free ourselves from the idea that babies are bad and have to be corrected. Others are hampered by the idea that babies are toys to fulfill our own needs and not persons. These notions result in the warping of personality. Then, of course, there are many cases of outright neglect and rejection by persons who are sufficiently developed physically to reproduce but who have never developed much beyond the infantile stage psychologically. When a personality is crippled and warped, the damage does not end with the individual, because he or she breeds and warps, breeds and warps, in an endless chain.

Many children who have had unfortunate infancy could be helped back on the road to normal living if they could come in contact with really good people after they are old enough to go to school. Many psychologists will deny this, saying that the damage to the unloved infant is irreparable. I suppose this is true if we think of complete recovery. But these damaged children can be helped by high quality living in the schools. Howard Lane has said that no child ever became a serious delinquent who had one genuine adult friend whom he could really trust. This is probably too sweeping, but it is, I believe, substantially true. There are some children who, if they are to have such a friend, will find that friend in the teacher. There is no other adult available to them. We might think that this adult friend ought to be the parent, but often this is impossible. The parent or parents have already damaged the child. And besides, it is more difficult for a parent to fill this role than it is for another person. There is apt to be an enormous amount of emotional content in the parent-child relationship, which makes the real friendship situation unmanageable.

This friendship has to be real, hard, and firm. The adult must avoid talking down to the child or youth. He must not be condescending, or appear in the role of the all-wise. Here are two people of different ages who have established a human bond. They will not discuss matters which are beyond the understanding of the child; neither will the adult talk baby talk. In brief, the adult shall not be a "phony" in any way. The friendship must be on the level of complete sincerity. Any deviation from this will be detected immediately by the child, and the bond will begin to dissolve.

Soft kindness and fatherly advice may do more harm than good. Twenty-five or thirty years ago my work took me into juvenile court a good deal. The judge was a kindly old gentleman who believed that all any boy needed was to have a good lecture from the judge on the error of his ways and then to be treated with kindness. It was just at the time when radios were being developed that could be plugged in, instead of relying on batteries. A radio manufacturer in town had a large supply of sets requiring batteries, and the judge acquired a good many of them because they had become obsolete. After the delinquent boy had listened to the judge's lecture he was released and presented with one of these radios. The radio was, of course, worthless until the boy secured a battery. There followed a rash of stolen automobile batteries all over town. The cause was traced to the judge's gifts.

There are many good adults among our teachers, but here again we get our means and ends mixed up. Instead of starting to nurture and to repair damage through recognition of each child's unique needs and damages, we are obsessed with adult ends. We have an obsession, for example, with the notion that every child, no matter what his condition, shall learn to read when he is six years old. Scientific research tells us that this is impossible, but we pay no attention. Regardless of his condition, we start beating him over the head about something which in many cases has no meaning to him. We are so anxious to convince the world that we have high standards that we are now greeting the five-year-old, when he comes into kindergarten, with something we call "reading readiness." As though readiness could be taught and is not a product of growth! So hysterical have we become about this matter that we are led to wonder whether or not parents procreate in order to have a reader rather than a child.

I use our attitude toward reading only as an example. I want as many as possible to learn to read as much as they can, when they can. Reading is a great tool which can add much to the richness of living, and I cherish it for everybody. By being hysterical about it, however, and feeling that our own pride is at stake, we create reading problems where few need to exist. I feel sure that the pressure for adult ends is one way in which delinquents are made.

Frequently someone gets tied up in statistics and announces to the astonishment of all that most crimes are committed by youth under twenty-one. The papers never get tired of printing this, and the public is always properly shocked This is good for a play about once every three years. Certainly most crimes are committed by youth. What would one expect? The whole crime problem is really a youth problem. Nearly all criminals are warped and damaged in childhood and youth. Very few people over twenty-one set out to commit their first crimes. Some few do, under great provocation or during times of mental ill health, but almost every adult criminal has a history of behavior during his childhood and youth which reveals early damage to his psychological self. The breeding place for adult crime is in the cradle of the unwanted, the unloved, the unassimilated.

Having produced delinquents, we often err in our treatment of them. We have improved a good deal since the days when children were treated as adult criminals, but we still cling pretty much to the punishment and atonement concept. Some people who deal with delinquents make the mistake of the judge described above. Others go to the opposite extreme of demanding vengeance. The vagaries of the judges in juvenile cases cause some odd things to happen. Their religious and racial prejudices are often a factor. Often a delinquent needs a whole new environment which can be provided only by being placed in a foster home. One judge I know about believes that "there's no place like home," so he refuses to use foster homes but insists that the youth be returned to the very place that damaged him in the beginning. The adulation of "home" is deep in American culture, but sometimes the youth's home is a cesspool of filth, hate, and corruption. To return a delinquent to the environment which damaged him is asking for more trouble.

It must be said in defense of those who deal with delinquents that because of public apathy and penuriousness, they do not have room for the youth who are brought to them and who need a different environment. I have heard police in Detroit complain because when they take a wayward youth to the detention home, he gets back to the neighborhood before the police can. But our facilities are so outgrown that there is little else the officials can do. We need many more good foster homes, but the county pays so little for the support of children sent to foster homes that most people feel that they cannot afford to take children. With so little support money the aides of the court have a difficult time preventing the approval of foster homes where exploitation of children is the motive. Penury is apt to call forth the lowest forms of life.

I hasten to pay tribute to many foster parents who take unfortunate children at a financial loss and nurture them because they love children. Often these people finally adopt some of these children and surround them with the full status and love due their own. What a wonderful thing it would be if there were enough of such people.

When a young person does something which is not acceptable to our culture, particularly if a policeman happens to come along, he is caught in a downward spiral which tends to produce more anti-social behavior. The full force of the opprobrium of his society descends upon him. Gossip mongers take over, and the youth's whole world collapses around him. His parents often care more about their "good name" and what the delinquent has done to them than about their own young. And this horrible act may have been something that he got into quite innocently. To be sure the act is probably one which ought not be condoned, but it is not one which deserves the withdrawal of love and support by parents, neighbors, teachers, and other adults who make up his world.

The school sometimes takes the lead in pointing the finger of scorn. There is a good chance that the offender will have to listen to a lecture from the principal on the subject of bringing discredit to the school. On top of all that has happened he is cast in the role of the black sheep and is shunned by all "good" boys and girls. He may even be expelled from school, because "one rotten apple spoils the whole barrel." If he is not expelled, he is likely to be denied all of the "privileges" of the school. This means that he can no longer participate in those things at school which he has enjoyed most, and his absence from them and his presence in the study hall makes him all the more conspicuous. This is un-American, for he has to pay for the same crime three times—once with the judge, police or probation officer, once in his home and neighborhood, and again at school.

It is hard for the ordinary adult to realize what it means to a teenager to have his world collapse in this fashion. It is not unlike what happened to the lepers of old or to the untouchables of old India. Of course, the whole matter is not as serious as it seems to the youth, and the day may come when, as a paunchy middle-aged man, he may brag about what a devil he was. But we make the youth feel that because of this mistake, his world has really come to an end.

Such feelings of degradation are apt to increase anti-social behavior rather than reduce it. Ordinary logic would tell us that this would be true. If one sees himself as an outcast, he thinks he has nothing to lose. So, caught in the downward spiral, more such behavior is likely to follow. There comes a time when the judge feels forced to commit him, if there is room for him, to what is called a school. In Michigan this is called the Vocational School; in Wisconsin it is named the Industrial School. At any rate, the name is deceiving. Although the personnel in these "schools" usually do the best they can with the niggardly resources available to them, the schools are little more than jails. They *could* be better than jails, but it would cost more money. We do not care that much what happens to our young. Anyway they are not *our* young—just some riffraff. At least this is true until the lightning strikes our house.

Some youth are so badly damaged, so sick, that they have to be confined for their own safety and the safety of the public. There surely is a better way, however, than building jails for them. I believe that something irreparable happens to any boy or girl when the door to the cell clicks shut. All self-respect, all identity as a person, departs. Perhaps the most traumatic moment in such a life is when the policeman first says "Come with me." This is sometimes necessary, but we ought to know what it is we do and do it the best way we can, ameliorating its effects as much as possible.

When a youth is put in jail he is probably mentally ill, at least to a degree before this happens. He is thus confined where his only company is others who are also mentally disturbed. And so these youths live together sharing their quirks. When we consider that one has to have good people in order to improve in such a jam, it is easy to see what harm is done by confinement and association with youth in a similar plight. The grip of the whirlpool is now almost complete. Reconstruction becomes most unlikely.

Many of us still seem to be obsessed with the idea of retribution, that one must "pay for his sins." These youth jails used to be called "reform schools," as though they ever reformed anybody. I do not believe that anybody, adult or young, ever came out of such an experience better than he was when he went in. From the very nature of the situation, and from what we know about how adequate people are built, it is hard to see how anyone could be thus improved. Some adult criminals reach the point where they cannot be further damaged, but this is not true of the young. Society has to be protected, of course, but we need to think this whole matter through anew. We need to get rid of the old notion of retribution and begin to think of constructive processes. We need to become willing to pay enough to attempt to undo the evil we have done.

The best way to prevent delinquency is to stop producing delinquents. This is not a very practical suggestion, but it helps to clarify the fact that delinquents are in almost every case made by adults. There are very few who are defective at birth. When we see a teen-age boy who is so hostile that he is inaccessible—he hears nothing anybody says to him—it is a sobering thought to realize that he was all right when we got him and that if he is hostile and inaccessible now, it is due to what has happened to him in an adult-managed world over which he had no control.

We cannot stop producing delinquents altogether because we cannot control the birth of the unwanted and unloved. Much of the damage, though not all, is caused in infancy. We might in time do away with poverty and slums, although these are not direct causes of delinquency. If these running sores in our society could be eliminated, we would have a better chance to raise a generation of people who are basically loving in their attitudes toward others. Such people would not be apt to produce so many of the unloved and unwanted.

Granting that for the foreseeable future we will always have some of our young in conflict with society, we must now think how we can deal with them more constructively. Too many of them now get worse rather than better after the first detected incident. We can find ways of reducing the opprobrium which all segments of society now too often hold for them. Perhaps we will have to modify our concept of sin and retribution. Since no one is qualified to cast the first stone, maybe we ought to stop casting them. It seems especially ironic for us to expect a youth to "pay his debt to society" when we ourselves are the real culprits. When a youth has been damaged beyond repair, the debt society owes is beyond computation. If he is run over by an automobile driven by a negligent driver, the courts have rules for assessing damage—so much for an eye, so much for a leg, and so on. But we have no formula for the damaged self, also brought about by irresponsible adults. The culprit is never insured against this kind of recklessness.

The fact remains that the amount of delinquency in any community is a direct measure of that community's concern for its young.

Chapter 6

What Does Youth Need of Us?

A Real Place in Our Society

Youth needs, first of all, a bona fide place in our society. This means a place where he feels that he is really needed, that he is pulling his weight in the boat, that his effort would be missed if he did not do so. As it is now he hears a good deal about how much he costs and very little about how much he is needed. He passes through a long period when he must feel himself to be a burden on society. The school he attends is grudgingly supported, and the newspapers carry stories and editorials on the awesome cost of education. He goes to his class and finds that there are about ten more students in it than can be properly managed. He cannot help thinking that if he were not there it would help some.

The studies that are imposed upon him often make no sense to him at all. That being the case, even though he gives it a good try, he is met by failure and defeat. It is not long until he sees that his absence would be a matter of deep gratification to his teachers and school officials. So he decides that school is not a bona fide place for him. It may be all right for the students who understand such matters, but not for him.

If he then turns to the world of work, he finds it pretty well blocked for reasons already stated. What he can find to do, if anything, is certainly not very essential, and he cannot escape the fact that society could make out very well without him.

At home he has been led to believe that everything there belongs to his parents. This idea has been nurtured as far back as his memory goes. For example, in our more affluent homes where there is a lawn, he has been paid to mow it. This means that it is not his lawn, for obviously no one should be paid to mow his own lawn. And so it is with the other things around the home. They are not his, and so he can't feel responsible for them. He is apt to feel that he is actually a guest in his own home, and sometimes he feels that he has worn out his welcome.

No one ever became a real part of anything unless he felt needed and consulted. Our young people are a misplaced segment of our society. It will require changes in our schools to make them so that no one will depart at the close of the day without the feeling that the school ran better that day than it would have if he had stayed away. It is even more difficult to change the atmosphere of the home so that youth feels that he really belongs in it. This is made very difficult because of urbanization and mechanization, so that there is little in the home to be responsible for or in which to feel ownership. The problem of employment in its true sense becomes harder every year with production going up and employment going down. All of these problems must be faced if we are to make a genuine place for our young in our society.

Good Recreation Helps

Young people have a great deal of energy which has to be spent in one way or another. It is almost boundless. This energy was formerly spent in a natural way, in farm work, fighting the elements, walking long distances to school, and so on. When we moved into cities, we pent up this energy by living in small houses, apartments, and, too often, in slums. It comes about that every city block is literally bursting with the unspent energy of our young.

One answer to this problem is the providing of recreational facilities in considerable quantity and often in good quality. We have a good many playgrounds. Schools have gymnasiums, although they are often locked after school hours. Many communities support "teen canteens," places where youth can go to spend an evening with their friends playing indoor games. In many cities there are boys' clubs, offering many activities in the evening, both active and sedentary. These are usually operated by dedicated adults who genuinely like young people.

There are not enough of these facilities, as one can see when he considers than in a big city like Detroit, for example, there are hundreds of thousands of youth. Cities have devoted some of their precious space to parks and playgrounds, but not enough, and these facilities are apt to be located near the more privileged youth and far from the ones that need them most. This has not been done to show partiality, but it is easier to establish a park on the outer edges of a city than it is to clear space for one in a blighted area.

I do not mean to deprecate the many efforts which have been made to provide recreation for our young. Private individuals have given of their resources, in some cases all they have had, because they really cared. We have even spent considerable tax money (the last full measure of devotion) for this purpose.

Besides being too little and too late, there are other reasons why our recreational facilities have fallen short of our expectations in solving the problems of youth. First, young people do not want to play all of the time. They want to be a significant part of the community. The very fact that the community says in effect "Now you go and play; see what a nice place we have fixed for you" is a rejection of a sort. What we are saying is "Get out of our way, so that the important things of life may go on."

Second, the fact that "we have fixed a nice place for you" has caused the failure of many of our efforts. Adults plan places for youth to recreate without ever thinking that youth might have been consulted. Many times adults are puzzled and grieved because they have spent their money for a playground, and almost no young people go near it. "What in the world do these kids want?" we cry in anguish. The fact that adults do not know how to plan for youth and that youth have been excluded from the planning never occurs to us. The implication is that the young are incapable of making sensible suggestions.

It must be said, unfortunately, that some adults undertake recreational activities for youth for their own purposes. Whenever a private individual begins to spend money in this way, it is a good idea to look at his motives. For example, if an individual or a corporation really wants to help young people, it will not be necessary to have the company's name on the backs of those who are being "helped." There are other examples of the exploitation of youth under the guise of recreation. Even scholastic and collegiate football are primarily not played for fun any longer. Many a boy, because he has ability to "play," is forced through social pressure to go through long hours of drill when he would prefer to be getting an education. At the same time he is expected to do his homework and keep his grades up. This is not for him but for "dear old alma mater."

Dear old alma mater is personified by the coach, who wants a bigger job, the school officials whose jobs are pretty secure as long as the team wins fame, and the alumni who like a Roman holiday and see themselves as making the touchdowns personally. If a capable youth wants to retire from this arena, it is considered an impertinence. He is called upon to "die for dear old Siwash," and occasionally he does. Surely he must often feel that others are giving his life away rather lightly and freely. The exploitation of youth for adult purposes still goes on, often in the guise of recreation. Young people usually see through it and resent it.

The boundless energy of youth, pent up by city living, its expenditure thwarted by the fact that more and more of the work of the world is done by machinery, has to have a constructive outlet. Recreation alone, though helpful, is not enough. The city home could consume some of it but cannot really meet this need. As we look at our social structure, we see only one institution which could supply what youth has been deprived of by urbanization and mechanization. That is the public school.

The School as Youth Center

The American public school is one of the greatest inventions in the history of man. This is not to say that there are not good public schools elsewhere. But this country is the only large one which has undertaken the education of all who will partake of it through the twelfth grade. We have believed that education for all is essential to the successful operation of a democracy; that we cannot afford an illiterate electorate. We have backed this belief by making a high school education available to every boy and girl in the land. It may mean a long journey by bus for some, but we have furnished the transportation. These educational opportunities are not equally good for all as yet, but we are now working on that. We do not believe that the accident of birth, whether it be remote geographically or whether it be a matter of race or creed, should deprive a citizen of his right to an education. We are presently resolved that in the matter of equal educational opportunity there shall be no second class citizens, no educationally disinherited.

The concept of secondary education for all came as a natural consequence of urban living. It was the result of the American dream, which was that if not everybody could be President, anybody might be; that regardless of the circumstances under which any American was born, he had the inherent right to try to better himself, and that there is no limit to the extent one might improve his condition except his own limitations. In addition there was the problem of having youth with time on their hands, due to urbanization, and the pressure for jobs among adults. This pressure resulted in the passage of child labor laws which restricted youth from seeking employment. Not all child labor laws were enacted for the good of youth, but they resulted in the necessity of schools for everyone.

The idea of education for all began to be a reality at about the close of World War I. The modern secondary school started in about 1920 and grew until about 1940. So we can see that it is a relatively young institution. We now have a huge institution with many buildings and many teachers, costing the American taxpayers a great deal of money. Beautiful new buildings are being built all over the United States. It is an institution of such magnitude and with such great potential for good that we can feel fortunate indeed to have it.

In the very nature of the way the secondary school came about, it should be a youth center where the needs of all youth could be met. It should be a place toward which any youth who feels at loose ends would turn. He would go there naturally because he would know that there he would meet friendly adults and could acquire friendly peers. He would know that whatever his bent, there would be something that he could do and somebody who cared what became of him. If he could use nuclear physics or Shakespeare, it would be available. If he needed less abstract and more physical opportunities, they would be there, and he would be as highly respected in either case.

Here he could be initiated into the working world through what is called the work-study plan. Some schools do this now, but not enough do. This would be of enormous value to youth and of as much value to the adult population. Every employer in town ought to share in this program. He should be treated as a part of the educational system of the community. If the employers were taken in on the education of youth and saw themselves as educators, if they were used and consulted, they would become more understanding and more friendly. Then it would be possible for schooling and employment to merge in the life of the youth. So often, if the youth stays around until graduation, he is turned out amid a display of carnations and oratory without any concept of what the working world is like.

If the school were really a youth center, it would be the school's reason-to-be. Here we could make up to youth what we took away when we became industrialized and all moved as close together as we could get. Here could be his opportunity for learning to assume responsibility. Here the lessons of citizenship could be learned by living in, and helping to operate, the society which a school constitutes. There is no place else in an urban culture where these learnings, once a natural part of living, can be cultivated.

Of course, there are a good many other places for youth in our society besides the school. Many churches do a great deal for youth and really hold out a welcoming hand to them. Organizations for boys and others for girls do fine work. But the trouble with most of these is that they do not reach everybody, and often they reach only the ones who need them the least. Some organizations even keep their escutcheons clean by not admitting "bad" boys and girls. Some boast that their boys never become delinquent, having been careful not to admit a boy who they think will become so. The school is the only institution where all, through taxation, pool our resources to do a job for youth. It is the only place where youth is required by law, up to a certain age, to be in attendance. It can be our youth-centered institution.

It is not my intention at this point to say very much about the school. This is a long and complicated story. Now we are dealing with the situation in which youth finds itself in 1960. It seems important, however, to point out that our secondary schools, where all youth should thrive, fall far short of being really youth centered institutions.

This we can see by the fact that youth leave our schools by the thousands as soon as legally possible. A good many remain a while after they are legally free to go. Only about fifty per cent of those who finish the eighth grade graduate from high school. This figure varies with communities and may not be very accurate. There are many ways of gathering statistics. But whatever the figure may be, it is enormous.

Then there are thousands more who really drop out in all but the physical sense. We have little knowledge of the actual dropouts from our high schools, because all we know how to do is to count the bodies. Many a dropout is still in school. But if we consider only those who have left school physically, the figure is staggering. Dropping out of school would not be so serious were it not that our young really have nowhere else to go.

It has been estimated from population figures that in a city the size of Detroit there are 50,000 young people who have left school and are really at loose ends. (I mention Detroit not because it is worse in this regard than other large cities. It is the one I know best.) We have no idea what these young people are doing. They are unknown to any agency. We know that they are not well employed, because the laws prohibit this. They may have some small fringe jobs, like working as newsboys. In the recent past some of them worked in bowling alleys, but now even pin setting is done by machine. Anyway this was not very desirable employment. Incidentally, there must be something peculiarly unsatisfying in setting up bowling pins only to have one's handiwork smashed as soon as it is completed—work done in order that it may be smashed. With fifty thousand youth on the loose we need not be surprised that some of them form gangs and indulge in anti-social behavior. It is remarkable that more of them do not.

For such a young person to turn to the school in his extremity is almost unheard of. They do not turn toward that which they have already repudiated. The reason that they do not turn to the school is because it is an adult institution with adult purposes. The program of the school consists of what we think youth ought to have. It is often dominated by college requirements, made up by people who do not even live nearby, whom the youth will never see, but who nevertheless seek to control their lives. A finely geared and oiled system of rewards and punishments to produce conformity to adult values is already in operation.

So the institution which should be youth's own often repels instead of attracts youth. Nobody voluntarily seeks out a situation where his purposes will be supplanted by the purposes of someone else. He does not return to that from which he has made his escape.

To make the school a genuine youth center will require rethinking the whole program, asking ourselves what best contributes to the needs of youth. This cannot, I believe, ever be done by adults alone. We cannot know the real feelings of youth because we are not young, and for that matter, most of us never grew up in an urban situation. We can only rethink the program of the school in consultation with and cooperation with youth themselves. This source is readily available.

I'd like to live to see the day when a young person, displaced and with time on his hands, will go to the school instead of the gang on the corner or in the drug store or pool hall. He will go to the school because there he will feel he belongs, that it is a second home, that all will be glad to see him and his need for others will be assuaged.

Another great need of youth is to have many adults concerned about them in a political sense. This should, of course, include everybody, but lacking this each community should have a group of adults who, throughout their lives, are organized to see to it that youth gets a fair deal in the political pull and haul that go on in our city, state, and national legislative bodies.

A democracy operates largely through pressure groups. Lobbying for special legislation is a recognized and legalized aspect of our society. A great deal of money is spent by manufacturers, real estate operators, doctors, lawyers, labor, and even by teachers to influence legislation to their own benefit. In times past and even now in some states so far as I know, lobbyists even went on the floor of legislative bodies to work for their particular interests.

I do not believe that the operation of these pressure groups is necessarily evil. It is the way by which our governments can be made to work. Pressure groups counterbalance each other so that as a rule no group can have its way entirely. It is my right as a citizen to get as much support as possible for any idea I may have for the improvement of the legal structure of my city and state. Our state is so large that no individual can have much influence by himself. If I wanted a law passed, I would first try to get as many people to agree with me as possible, to bring their collective influence to bear, and perhaps even to organize, collect money, and employ a lobbyist. If I could not get anybody to agree with me, it is unlikely that I could get very far with my idea.

Youth Needs Adult Pressure Groups

What I wish to point out is that youth constitutes a large segment of our society and has many needs. But they cannot themselves form a pressure group as other groups might. They cannot do it because of their youth and the way they live. They cannot vote (concerning which more will be said later), and so they cannot influence representatives. The status of being a youth is temporary—they soon become adults—whereas one can be a Mason or a Legionnaire, for example, for his whole adult lifetime.

This means that we have a large segment of people in our society who are with us but not of us. They are unrepresented in our government, except as they are represented by others. They suffer taxation without representation. They are our politically disinherited.

Because being young is temporary and because of youth's lack of power at the polls, they can hardly be expected to shift for themselves politically. I was tempted to include "because of their immaturity" in the above sentence, but then I thought of the social maturity of some of the members of our adult pressure groups and did not want to malign our teen-agers. The only way that seems open to us to make democracy work is for adults to espouse the cause of youth continuously and vigorously. This seems to me to be the clear duty of every American voter. It is asking a good deal, because I never heard of a pressure group which was not selfishly motivated, and this calls for pressure groups operating in the interest of someone else.

What We Have Tried in Detroit

It seems to me that youth will not get its fair representation in the tough arena of big city government and big state government unless there is an organized effort on the part of adults to insure it. In my own community (Detroit) considerable effort has been made to see that the interests of youth are represented. I know that many other large cities have made efforts along these lines. I write of Detroit because I know it best, and because I had some part in bringing these efforts about.

On June 21, 1943, the Detroit race riot occurred. Thirty-three persons were killed in our streets. It was without doubt the darkest day in our city's long history. From a human point of view, it was darker than the great fire, which burned the whole settlement to the ground, or the plague, which took the lives of most of the settlers. After this carnage social tensions were high, and somehow a good deal of the blame was credited to youth. The papers were full of accounts of delinquency, although it was a known fact that where Negro and white youth attended school together and knew each other, there was no trouble. When adults fail they look for a scapegoat, and the scapegoat is likely to be our own young. The riot was primarily an adult affair.

Having come recently from a thrilling experience with youth (see Part II) and being a teacher of high school teachers as well as supervisor of secondary education in Detroit, I was deeply concerned about the youth of the city. I was concerned about the stories of what seemed to me to be mishandling of youth by our police. There were about half as many police in Detroit at that time as there were teachers, and next to the teacher and the parent, the police had most contact with youth. Though we thought it necessary for teachers to understand youth, no one seemed to think it mattered that police were for the most part ignorant of such matters. Police contact with youth was too often antagonistic, and youth, through fear and rejection, were made worse rather than better.

My first thought was that we needed someone in our police department to teach our officers something about youth and how to be more helpful, less harmful, in our neighborhoods. Of course I had to have help from someone in government or someone near government who knew those who would have to be reached. I presented my idea to Mr. Donald Slutz, who was then and still is director of the Traffic Safety Association of Detroit. Mr. Slutz had been a city hall reporter for the Detroit *News* and had served as City Controller with Mayor Edward J.

Jeffries, Jr. He was and is a man of great social sensitivity, willing to give freely of his time and effort to bring about improvements.

Mr. Slutz succeeded in interesting Mayor Jeffries and Police Commissioner John F. Ballenger in trying some education for police in their dealings with youth. Both the mayor and the commissioner were deeply concerned that there be no recurrence of the race riot, and were therefore open to suggestions. Mr. Ballenger was particularly impressed when we pointed out to him that our city charter says that it shall be the duty of the police department to prevent crime as well as to apprehend criminals.

With Mr. Slutz doing the selling, we eventually employed Dr. Howard Lane, psychologist from Northwestern University, to become psychologist for the police department.* He instructed police in the ways of youth and in the importance of the contacts of the police with youth. His work resulted in the foundation of what was first called the Crime Prevention Bureau, later renamed the Youth Bureau. It has been and still is very successful. There is a central office where youth who are in difficulty with the law are brought. Officers there try to straighten out these difficulties without taking the youth to the Juvenile Court or to jail. There is at least one policeman in every precinct who is officially known as a youth officer and to whom young offenders are referred.

I believe that the Youth Bureau has substantially improved the condition of that segment of Detroit youth which comes to the attention of the police. This is, however, a small percentage of the youth living in our city. In addition to this we needed an organized group of adults who continuously concerned itself with the welfare of the young people who reside in our city. This group needed to be set up and supported by the city government so that it would have strong governmental support. It needed to be free of the influence of any agency other than government.

There was established, therefore, an organization called The Mayor's Committee on Children and Youth. It was composed of nine citizens appointed by the mayor. Its first meeting was held in January, 1951.† It was charged with the responsibility of keeping the welfare of all youth continuously before it and with bringing its influence to bear on the im-

* When I speak of my part in these matters, I should make it clear that I was only the catalyzing agent. Mr. Slutz, Dr. Lane, several police commissioners, and many others did the work.

† "The Lane Report" by Howard Lane is on file with the Detroit Commission on Children and Youth. This report was used by Mayor Cobo in establishing the Commission.

provement of this condition. It was to be concerned with all aspects of our society which affect youth. How fare Detroit youth? How are the social agencies functioning in this regard? Are our laws regarding youth effective and helpful? What happens to orphans?—to babies who are dependent on the public? Are youth being exploited? What about our schools and our courts? Are recreational facilities adequate? Do we as a community cherish our young? Are young lives being crippled by our neglect? Are we as a community contributing to our own delinquency problem?

The committee was granted a budget from public funds which enabled it to employ an executive secretary and a skeletal staff. Offices were provided at public expense. The committee met monthly and held special meetings as needed. In 1955 it was made a city commission by an act of the Common Council. It was then named The Detroit Commission on Children and Youth. Being elevated to the status of a commission was an important step, because as long as it was a mayor's committee, it could be abolished by any mayor at any time. The first executive secretary developed a large number of subcommittees, involving perhaps a hundred citizens at any given time. Many of these sub-committees worked long hours and did a great deal of good.

I was chairman of the committee from its inception in January, 1951, to July, 1955. I speak of this body in the past because I have not been connected with it since 1955. The commission is still operating, so far as I know. My last achievement with regard to it was to have it established as a city commission.

Speaking primarily from my firsthand knowledge of the committee, I feel that it has fallen short of my expectations, although much has been done. The committee was not militant and zealous enough to accomplish what I had hoped. We did not want to step on anybody's toes, and there were toes everywhere. I write these words with great reluctance, because I was most fond of every member of the committee, and I have no desire to offend any of them. My hope is that if another city attempts to emulate Detroit, it will be able to avoid the pitfalls we fell into.

I believe that the basis on which the mayor chose the committee was faulty. It was basically political, since all mayors have to have a weather eye out for political implications. The members were chosen with regard to whom they represent so that no cultural or ethnic group would be omitted. The question, I fear, was not how do these people feel about youth, nor how free are they, but how might they affect the vote when the mayor faced re-election.

To show what I mean, we had the following membership: (1) A representative of the juvenile court, (2) An executive of the YMCA, (3) A prominent layman in Jewish affairs, (4) Past president of the Detroit Federation of Women's Clubs, (5) Executive secretary of the Catholic Youth Organization, (6) Director of the Urban League, (7) A representative of big business, and (8) Director of the Detroit city budget, apparently appointed to check expenditures. I was the ninth member, put on because I had started the whole operation.

I cannot emphasize too much the high quality of these members, or the high regard in which I held each one. But they all had special interests other than youth. It was hard to find something to do which would not affect someone of them in his own work.

The mayor, the late Albert E. Cobo, had no idea that these conflicts of interest would arise. (Actually they did not arise, they merely existed.) He automatically thought in political and representational terms. Perhaps if this had not been his habit, he never would have been mayor. He did many things to help the committee and me. As a citizen I did not always agree with his political ideas, but in my role as chairman of the Committee on Children and Youth he gave me excellent support. He helped me defend our budget against the budget bureau; he helped untangle red tape with the civil service officials.

Being a governmental agency carries certain hazards. We had great difficulty securing staff because of the lack of pliability and the slowness of the civil service people. They even gave an inappropriate examination to one applicant because they did not have a suitable one on hand. The tight budget under which we operated kept us from doing many things which we should have done. For example, we had to make a special issue and secure the intervention of the director of the city budget to pay travel expenses for a man who lived in Madison, Wisconsin, whom we wanted to interview for the position of executive secretary. We had to anticipate what we wanted to do for youth about eighteen months in advance if it cost any money. The committee has had a series of executive secretaries, some of whom left out of sheer governmental frustration.

All this does not mean that the group of citizens charged with the welfare of youth should not be under government. I think it *has* to be, because if it were not, little attention would be paid to it. I mean merely to point to some of the weaknesses and pitfalls involved in being a governmental agency. There are none of these problems that could not be solved or prevented if governmental officials saw them and tried to prevent them. I do not think that any governmental official deliberately tried to frustrate the committee. They simply did not comprehend our problems; therefore they could not prevent them. Government, then, along with all other citizens, has to be deeply concerned about the welfare of youth and believe that the body representing youth is one of their most important ones.

What does youth need of us? He needs a genuine place in our society where he will feel needed. He needs organized adult pressure groups to represent him in the political fray, that he may not be excluded from the operation of our democracy. He needs a place either in school, in employment, or in college. He needs a place where he can recreate, but not as the most important of his activities. One recreates in order to be freshened for more important activities. He needs to feel that he is valued for himself, not exploited for adult ends.

How Shall We Live With Our Young?

As set forth earlier, one of the saddest aspects of our culture is that we do not know how to live properly with our young. Usually we love them when they are babies and as long as they are "cute." But when they grow gangling, acquire acne, and are filled with energy, we become annoyed with them. We have our own purposes for them, and this naturally leads to conflict. We are not at peace with them.

We need to clear up some misconceptions we hold about youth. For example, every young person wants an orderly society as much as we do. He wants a decent home and a good school which he feels belongs in part to him. He may rebel against what he feels to be the other person's home or school.

Contrary to the opinion of most adults, youth is idealistic. It is, in fact, the most idealistic time in most persons' lives. We often assume that if youth are not carefully watched, they will immediately become involved in taboo sex behavior and drunkenness. A few youth will do this, although they are considerably restrained by the mores of their peers. These few will probably find ways to behave thus, in spite of adult vigilance. The fact is that youth behavior in this regard is frequently much better than adult behavior. One needs only to go to an adult convention and then to a youth convention to see the difference. Most of us would be greatly refreshed by such an experience. After doing this, one might well raise the question as to who ought to be watching whom. To be sure adults should attend youth conventions if they want to or are needed. They should, however, be *with* youth, not *on* them.

One of the greatest needs of young people, indeed the greatest, is to live in an atmosphere of love. They need the love of all adults within their reach. We must think about what conditions of living in home and school make love possible. We need to identify the attitudes and concepts which are often held and which make love impossible.

It seems clear that we must adopt the cooperative way of life in home and school because love cannot thrive in authoritarian, competitive ways of living. The cooperative way of life is the means by which everyone may feel that he belongs, that he shares in the goods and the responsibilities of life. Without this feeling love will not flourish.

Below are some things which we need to bear in mind concerning our young when we think how we can live with them in cooperation, in peace, and in love.

1) He did not ask to be born. He was conceived (in both senses) by adults.

2) He had no control over the situation into which he was born. Even such an important matter as the color of his skin was not chosen by him.

3) He cannot make his own conditions of living.

4) He cannot represent himself in the give and take of political democracy.

5) Whatever he may be now, he was all right when we got him and is the product of the life he has led in an adult-managed world.

Part II

How citizens are made

Chapter 7

The Importance of Education for Citizenship

The state of being young is temporary. Our youth will grow up and in time will operate the affairs of the earth. As we will grow old, the reins will slip from our hands. The way youth are built will inevitably determine the shape of things to come. The school is our instrument for building our prospects. Since we have learned how to destroy all life, the very continuation of a human existence will be in their hands.

On August 6, 1945, over Hiroshima a new era came into being. The birth of the atomic age has outmoded most of our customary patterns of thinking. Many of our habits and institutions became obsolete over night. An era was born in which no man is safe except through the good will of all his fellow men. This calls for a brand of citizenship never before demanded of us.

How well prepared are we to meet this new challenge? Have we really been good citizens of the old outmoded world of 1944? How are we now motivated? Are we reacting as an informed and intelligent citizenry should react to a new situation? Do we have the feeling for the welfare of human beings so necessary to secure the good will we must have? Are we now responding in fear or in faith? In more crucial form than we could have imagined the test of what we fought for is now upon us. How are we meeting this test?

We are now given one more chance, perhaps the last, to see whether our ideals of citizenship can measure up to the needs of the hour. Do our youth, who get most of their ideals for cooperative living from our schools, know enough about democracy and cooperation to sustain them in a world so shrunken in size that we are all next-door neighbors? How do our youth feel about their own government and the welfare of their own people? How can they care about other peoples of the earth if they have not learned to care about their own? Do our youth know and appreciate what democracy is and what it means to live under the democratic system? Do they have an attitude toward democratic government that will sustain that government? Will they care enough about it to give their sweat and brawn to defend it in peace as well as in war?

The evidence that our youth do not understand and cherish the institutions of democracy is all about us. One has only to talk to the first ten high school graduates he meets to realize it. These high school graduates often think that democracy is something that gives them the right to do as they please and that our government is vaguely "pretty bad." Too often they look forward to pursuing a life as free from concern about government as possible.

The average adult American citizen is no better. We too often think of government in the third person. "That policeman is an enemy." "That fireman is a tax eater." The "government" is spoken of as some sinister thing which hangs over the citizens and busies itself in making their lives uncomfortable. Seldom does anyone speak of *his* government, *his* policeman, *his* fireman. All this in the face of the fact that the people created the government. The ironic fact is that the people mistrust and misunderstand the very instrument they invented and control. If the people could come to feel that they *are* the government, that it is theirs, and that they could control it, we would no longer have our malodorous city machines that return to power again and again with the tacit consent of good citizens. If the people felt that the government was theirs, we should no longer have our present public disdain of politics as being something dirty with which a decent citizen will have nothing to do. We would no longer have people talking about how life would perhaps be better if we had a dictator. In the dictator-blighted countries the dictators were turned to as an easy way to solve problems of work and security. Some of us were jobless so long that we began to think that an efficient dictator would give us work and security. We failed to realize that the only security worth having is that which we achieve for ourselves and not that which is given us by someone else.

If we have this lack of understanding of the nature of democratic living, wherein lies the failure in our preparation of youth for citizenship?

Much of the blame must be charged to the public schools. It is true that a young man or a young woman is a product of many influences of which the school is only one, but the great public school system, "the backbone of our civilization," "the foundation of the republic," had and has as one of its primary tasks that of building citizens. It has often been said that the chief reason why a childless taxpayer should support the schools his neighbor's children attend is that his benefits come from the development of good citizens; that if the neighbor's children should be allowed to grow up without the advantages of education, the childless taxpayer's life would be uncomfortable if not hazardous, and his whole economy would be threatened. Thus, the training of citizens is a primary and original charge upon the schools; and if we are not getting citizens equipped to live in a democracy, we are not getting our money's worth.

What kind of citizen does a democracy demand? It is not enough for the schools to develop just any kind of citizen. A special brand of citizenship is needed in a nation which is really of, by, and for the people. We need citizens who are excited about government, not apathetic or indifferent. We need citizens who will hold a bold, critical, inquiring eye upon their government, not obey its edicts with blind docility. We need critical thinkers and energetic doers and earnest devotees of democracy. These are the chief ends for which school taxes are paid in America.

The teaching of government and the training of citizens is the primary charge upon the schools, because the government is the implement which makes possible the use of all other knowledge. It is useless to learn science, for example, if the government does not permit free inquiry. The great Jewish physicians of Vienna had little use for their knowledge under Nazi control, because the government did not permit them to practice. We build and maintain our government so that we can live, as nearly as possible, the kind of life we consider desirable. The government, therefore, must be right *first,* then all other knowledge and skills can be useful. The American people have a right to demand that the schools make this their first business.

Our schools are again filled with millions of young people; people who will have terrifying responsibilities, if we hope to have peace. What are some of the attitudes our graduates must have if democracy is to be understood and sustained?

They must know first of all that democracy is a way of life, an attitude of man toward man, a dynamic changing force that is kept going by constant attention. They must know that it is not a thing apart. It is not something that George Washington secured for us and that resides in the Capitol. They should further know that democracy is the only way so far discovered which permits man to live his own personal philosophy. There is no other way of life so far demonstrated in which it is not necessary for some men to be masters and some to be slaves. It is the only way of life so far devised which permits the full development of the personality. Under the master-slave arrangement fear is the predominating factor in human life. Fear drives people within themselves so they do not dare say what they think or do what they wish, and their personalities dwindle and fade and die. To cherish and defend democracy, then, is to cherish and defend all we hold as decent and worthwhile.

I think youth needs to know that our American government is not democracy, but rather the machinery for helping its people achieve democratic ideals. It is an attempt on the part of those who believe in democracy to provide a system that will bring about democracy. It is something that we ourselves created, hoping that existence under it would approach the kind of life we thought we wanted. It is not a system developed by somebody else to oppress us, and we certainly need not, in fact, be oppressed by our own device for realizing our ideals. Our youth must cease to mistrust and begin to believe in our own invention. We must begin to admit that this government is our own product and stop disowning it and complaining about it.

Our youth must realize that the government is in truth responsive to the will of the citizens. If we have bad government it is because we either do not understand this fact or do not care. Bad government cannot exist except as we permit it to exist. Government largely takes the form that its citizens want it to take. When a smug and self-righteous citizen draws himself up to his full height and says that he will have nothing to do with that dirty government, he becomes an agent of bad government. He becomes an unintentional saboteur of democracy.

Our youth must realize that if democracy is to work, good local government must be demonstrated. He needs to worry less about who is president of the United States and more about the wily ward heeler. Local government is the government that people see. Its often unsavory machinations have given many of our so-called good citizens their distaste and disgust for government. The average citizen never sees the federal or state government operate, but if the local government is filled with graft, if the taxpayers' money is taken and he gets little in return, if the alleys are dirty and the garbage is not collected, he is most likely to say that if this is democracy he wants none of it. If local government is efficient and serves the purposes for which the citizens founded it, and if by so doing it keeps constantly before the citizens a living example of democracy in action, the state and national governments are almost certain to function properly; but the citizen must realize that local government will not function well unless he demands it and does his part to secure it.

Our youth have shown on a thousand battle fields that they are not afraid to die. We have all learned by bitter experience the truth of the statement by Lewis Mumford that says: "a life sacrificed at the right moment is a life well spent, while a life too carefully hoarded, too ignominiously preserved, is a life utterly wasted." Willingness to defend a faith makes it real. But our young people must learn in school that the effective defense of democracy may be more difficult in peace than in war. The alertness which we can now instill in our present high school youth may be enough to defeat the insidious peacetime enemies of democracy.

Our Teachers Must Believe in Democracy

If this alertness is to be instilled in our young, we must have teachers who really believe in democracy. We must have teachers who have not forgotten how they came to be or what their debt is to the democratic ideal. Most of our teachers were born in a lower economic and cultural state than they now occupy. They are largely the sons and daughters of farmers and workers. But for their good fortune in being born in a democracy, they would have lived and died as peasantry and in poverty. This is the land which gave them the chance to better their condition, but more than that, this is the land that gave them hope, without which humans cannot become really human.*

Many of our teachers have forgotten the source of their power and have been using this power to damage the very ideals which have made them possible. If there is any group in America which should be grateful for America, it is our teachers. They have used the ladder which is basic to the American dream. We have teachers, however, who sneer at colleagues who try to introduce some democratic living into their classes. They block attempts to arrange any participation by students in the affairs of the school. They proclaim that no little brat is going to tell *them* what to do. They say "I've tried democracy, but it doesn't work." One wants to ask, "How did you get here, if it doesn't work?"

Ever since our schools were established they have been of great interest to the public. The value of what the school does has long been debated. This I believe to be good. It shows that the citizens are really interested in their schools. Magazines and newspapers would not print articles about the schools unless they thought that the public would be interested in them.

* To better understand how this works in some other countries, see Hadley Cantril, *The Politics of Despair* (New York: Basic Books, Inc., 1958).

Of all who have expressed an opinion on what the schools should teach or should be, there is probably no one who would not agree that a primary function of the school is to produce good citizens. There may be some who think it would be enough to have just a *few* good citizens, but I am sure no one would take issue with the general objective. They would disagree only with regard to what methods and subject matter produce good citizens.

The School Is a Society Where Democracy Can Be Practiced

I am taking the position here that the school is in itself a society with many of the problems of any society; that it is a ready-made society in which young people can learn how to be citizens by practice; that in order for anyone to become a good citizen he has to see himself as a citizen, he has to perceive himself as a person who is a factor in what goes on; that no one ever does anything voluntarily unless he sees it as worth doing; that the school is his school and that he can have some small influence on what it is.

For example, I consider myself to be a citizen of the state of Michigan. It is true that I cannot have my own way, and many things go on of which I do not approve. I am one among millions of others. But I do feel that if I had a cause and could get a good many people to agree with me, I could have it written into the law of the state. It is unlikely that I will ever do this, but the fact that I am not forbidden to do it is what makes me feel that I am in fact a citizen. Of course, I want the right to vote, but if I had no right to try to get those elected to behave as I think they should, citizenship would mean very little to me.

Do the youth in our schools feel that they are a part of it? Do they think they have any chance to alter what goes on? Do they have a feeling of involvement necessary to sustain their self-concept as citizens? Perhaps some of the most successful have these feelings, but what about Joe Doakes in the back seat? In a very few years Joe is going to vote on school bonds. Are we making some mistakes in what we believe makes citizens?

Chapter 8

Ideas Which Block Us

We Have Too Much Faith in the Power of Telling

I believe that the public and most of our teachers do have mistaken notions as to how good citizens are made. Let us examine some of them at this point.

We seem to have great faith in the value of telling people what they ought to do. If we could save the world by exhortation, everybody by now would be convinced of the life good to live and be living it, instead of being in constant fear that our very existence is about to come to an end. I don't suppose that there is a boy or girl in America who has not been told to be good. The girl in the song "I Can't Say No" sings "I've known what's right from wrong since I was ten." It has been said that the inhabitants of our penitentiaries can quote more scripture than those on the outside. (I suspect data of this sort, because they have had plenty of time since they came in to read scripture, and may have learned it on the spot.) I do not say that it never does anybody any good to be told, but I think the evidence is sufficient to say that lectures on citizenship are not to be depended on for the development of good citizens.

The reason that telling is so ineffective is that it does not involve the listener. He may not even be listening, although his face is upturned with an eager look. He may merely be fascinated by the lecturer's false teeth. Telling simply does not motivate behavior. A person does what he does because it seems logical and sensible to him. This is determined primarily by the way he sees himself in relation to the spot he is in.

This "telling" business is an enormous block. We all love to give advice, because the role of the advice-giver makes us feel superior. I would not give you advice if I did not think I was smarter than you. We keep at this year after year although we can see that people pay little or no attention to it. In fact, it may even impell them to do the opposite. Sometimes we jest about the futility of giving advice just before we "let them have it."

This is such a big block to the proper education of citizens because it seems so difficult to imagine the day when the flow of adult advice will be lessened, when we will use preaching and exhortation only as it will serve, and when we will learn that advice to youth can only be utilized when youth are ready to hear it.

We Have Great Faith in the Grading System As a Way of Inducing What We Call Good Citizenship

Here I shall confine my remarks to the practice of giving grades for citizenship. Often this induces the wrong kind of behavior if we want to develop thinking, problem solving people. What does it mean when your boy brings home an "A" in citizenship? Too often it means that he has been compliant and conformist in his behavior. He has done promptly what the teacher told him to do. It means that he has not annoyed the teacher by raising bothersome questions. It means that he has not been inventive or creative. He has not shared with his peers, because to do so would disrupt the class. A well trained conformist is ill-fitted to meet the problems of the rapidly changing world. Like it or not, education for conformity is not education for citizenship. It may even be education for the sanitarium. It is contrary to the fundamental nature of energetic, restless, creative youth.

Let us stop giving grades for citizenship, at least until we decide what good citizenship is, and develop some criteria for judging it. Let us cease giving rewards for values which merely make adults more comfortable and which strengthen the feeling that the school is really an adult institution created and operated for the benefit of adults.

We Are Obsessed by the Idea That a Good Way to Educate for Citizenship Is to Run a Contest

Citizenship contests almost always involve skill in either writing or speaking or both. These are skills which are not especially developed by school experiences. There are only a few in each school who can possibly see themselves as winning. Often *everybody* is required to participate, but only a few have the slightest chance of success. Whenever anybody undertakes anything, he has to see that success is at least remotely possible. To require anyone to enter an enterprise *in which he knows he* *cannot win* is to decrease rather than increase his feeling that he is part of what goes on.*

As I say, these contests almost always involve the same skill so that there is always a group of youth who have a chance and a group who have no chance. If we were to change the objective—if for example, we ran an all-school contest to determine who could build the best boat, or even the best privy—we would then have a new set of winners. This would not be good, because it is never good to do things which exclude many, but at least we would get a temporary glance at a new elite.

In no activity other than reading and speaking would we think of pitting everybody against everybody else. We do not expect everybody to make the football team. We do not ask our polio victims to make the track team. We do not have a standard that everyone, before graduation, must run a hundred yards in eleven seconds. We forget that people are unique in regard to writing and speaking as well as in running and jumping. And let us not lose sight of the fact that all of this is done because we believe it makes good citizens.

There seems to be a notion widely held that democracy and competition are inseparable and that by promoting competition we are, therefore, promoting democracy. If we look at the meaning of democracy, the integrity of the individual, the dignity of man, the worth and value of each unique human being, all of which most of us concede, it is hard to see what this has to do with competition or what competition in school can contribute to the development of the democratic citizen. The democratic citizen has to learn to love his fellow man and be concerned for his welfare. How this can be when he is pitted against his fellow man is hard to see.†

Even the winner of the essay contest is not thereby made a better citizen. He is automatically more separated from his fellows than he was before. The beaten ones do not love him more for beating them. If the winner is a potential leader, he is further separated from the ones he might lead.

Democracy and competition are related in the public mind, because most people think our economic system is pure, cold competition. Even if this were true, which I do not grant, it would mean only that we use competition as a method of distributing the goods of earth and not that

* See Arthur W. Combs, "The Myth of Competition" in *Childhood Education*, February, 1957.

† For a fuller treatment of the problem of cooperation and competition, see Chapter 9 of Kelley and Rasey, *Education and the Nature of Man* (New York: Harper & Brothers, 1952).

it has anything to do with the brotherhood of man. I doubt that anyone would contend that competition makes us love our brethren more. If this is true, how can it then be a useful device in the development of democratic citizens?

Many of the contests in our schools are sponsored by our lay organizations. The people in these groups have the best intentions. In fact, they appropriate money out of their dues because they want to be helpful. They have little to spare for what they call education, and about all they have enough for is to offer some contest prizes. Holding a contest is for them the easiest thing that they can do in education. I say "for them," because it is not so easy for those who have to enter the contest, or for the teachers who have to read and judge the papers.

Even though adults cherish this experience for others, they do not relish it for themselves. While I was supervisor of secondary education in Detroit, a member of one of the big service clubs of Detroit called me to say that the members of his group had a feeling that the young people of Detroit were being badly educated. He asked that every high school graduate of that year be required to take an examination which the club would devise. I told him that since there were thousands of graduates I doubted that it would be necessary for everybody to take the test but that there were sampling methods which would enable us to get the same information and that I would be glad to administer the test to such a sample on one condition. This was that each member of his club, or a suitable sample, take the same test. I never heard from him again.

The principals and teachers in the schools where these contests sponsored by outside organizations are run usually do not like them. They are not free, however, to refuse. The community groups (sometimes it is a newspaper) are very powerful and not to be offended lightly. The principal may know that this is not good education for citizenship but his community has to approve him. It is one thing to displease one parent but quite another to alienate an organized group or to get the power of the press arrayed against him. I sometimes think that the schools have little to lose by offending the press when it wants a contest since the press could hardly do more than it has done to lower public opinion of teachers and administrators.

Previously I have made the point that community organizations have the best of intentions when they sponsor contests. Since they do not understand such matters, it seems a good way to promote good citizenship, and they naturally have little money in this fund. If, however, instead of making a decision on their own and then bringing pressure to bear on school people, they would confer with the teachers and administrators they could do much more constructive things with small sums. They would then have professional advice about a professional matter. For example, a gift to the student council might in some cases make some very good things possible. There are many other places in any school where a couple of hundred dollars could be well spent to promote the life good to live, and thus promote good citizenship. We do not have to sponsor contests because only a small sum is available.

We Think That Special Awards Cause Good Citizenship

Perhaps the outstanding example of this is the honor societies of our secondary schools, although we now have honor societies in our junior high schools and may have extended them to the elementary schools. Many elementary schools have "awards days" at any rate. Of course, the college Phi Beta Kappa is well known. The high school honor society is a good example to show how extrinsic rewards operate. Even Dr. Conant,* although supporting the idea of the separation of the elite, sees the harm in these societies. His reason for objecting to them is not as strong as it might be but seems valid. He says that the students choose "soft" subjects in order to qualify. This is undoubtedly true not only in high school but in college as well. It is, in fact, a tribute to the intelligence of such students, for if the main objective is the grade, why not choose subjects concerning which one already knows a great deal? So perhaps, by the back door, we *do* get the brightest into these societies.†

The real objection to these societies is that they separate certain youth from their fellows and thus render them incapable of functioning as citizens. We need to weigh the effect of being chosen for the honor society and also the effect on those who tried hard but did not make it. Usually at an honors convocation there are tears shed by those who have been induced by adults to pursue false gods and have failed. There is also a large amount of indifference on the part of the rest of the youth who never saw themselves as among the elite and couldn't care less about the whole thing.

Of course, there are other criteria besides grades for being chosen for honor by adults. But most of these have to do with conformity in one way or another. They stress leadership, and it is as if to say, "You have

* James B. Conant, *The American High School Today* (New York: McGraw Hill Book Co., Inc., 1959).

† I question the idea that any course is soft in itself. It depends on the individual. If there were a course in baton twirling, it would be a "hard" course for me.

been a good leader, so we will remove you from those you might lead. You have been a good citizen, so we will build a barrier between you and other citizens with whom you need to cooperate."

Because of the differences between the sexes, there are many more girls than boys in honor societies. Girls mature earlier than boys, and hence are able on the whole to make better grades than boys, especially during the adolescent years. It seems to be in the very nature of things that girls are less aggressive than boys and more likely to conform, so that girls not only lead in what is called scholarship, but also in what is generally known as citizenship.

This peculiar screen we shake people through has some curious effects. One of the large corporations, I am told, has an unspent fund of eight million dollars set aside for scholarships for prospective engineers. This company wants the recipients to be in the top ten percent scholastically. It comes about that the top ten percent are mostly girls, and most of the few boys in this category do not want to be engineers or have already been grabbed off. So the eight million dollars remains almost intact. If the corporation or the school personnel knew how to discover the curious, the inventive, the restless, the nonconformist, they would locate our best prospects for engineers. But these nonconformists have already flunked the citizenship test.

I venture to say that nobody ever became a good citizen, in the proper definition of the term, by trying to get into a high school or college honor society. These organizations cannot be said to promote good citizenship. They often promote the lowest forms of behavior, the selections of courses one already knows, diminishing one's peers, and cheating on examinations. As a teacher-counselor, I have received the confessions of some of our "best" boys who had either been caught cheating and whose position in the whole world seemed about to crash, or whose consciences would no longer allow them to go on without telling someone. All in order to "make" the "honor" society. Thus we think we make citizens!

We Have Great Faith That a Course Can Make a Citizen

There is a law in the State of Michigan which requires that no one shall graduate from a high school without a course in American history or civics. Recently the Michigan legislature passed a law saying that no one in the state can be granted a degree of any kind without having had a course in political science. We witnessed the spectacle of people who had believed that they had completed the requirements for bachelor's, master's, or doctor's degrees being hauled back to take such a course. This was to make them better citizens.

Let no one think that it is here contended that there is anything wrong in such courses in themselves. That all depends on how the course is taught, since any course can contribute to making an effective citizen, and any course can deter it. The history requirement never was any problem since it is not ordinarily possible for anyone to go through four years of high school without being scheduled into a history course. One might ask whose history the legislature meant, since the history taught in Mississippi, for example, is probably different from that taught in Michigan. It is good to know as much as we can about our past, since it is the past and the future which make the present possible. But one can grow toward the ideals of the robber barons as well as toward the selflessness of a Lincoln. Then again, whose Lincoln? The demon who destroyed the South or the saint who preserved the union?

Civics courses are often laden with details not well related to one's concept of himself as a citizen. One doesn't become a good citizen to be required to memorize the salary of the drain commissioner or even the governor for that matter. It is true, of course, that a civics course could be so conducted that youth would come to value their country more. Even if this occurs, it is not the required course in civics that does it. Rather, it is a result of a learner coming in contact with a teacher who loves his country and can arrange experiences which will result in a similar feeling on the part of the learner. This should happen in all courses, not just in the civics class.

It is urgent that our young come into possession of a deep appreciation of not only the value of American citizenship but of world citizenship as well. Our young are distressingly ignorant of their own country as well as the rest of the world. This has been shown by many surveys. The Purdue surveys of high school student opinion reveal it—all of this after many years of required courses. If we could get it through our heads that requiring a course does not make a citizen, we could then ask ourselves what does. This would be a big step in advance.

This seems as good a place as any to say that any attempt by a legislature to establish specific school programs is likely to fail of its purpose. Legislators do not know about teaching and learning, so when they try to make decisions about such matters, they often miss their objective, however laudable. They have practically no other device than to fall back on required courses. Required courses often have the opposite effect from the one hoped for. For example, a required course in civics can as easily make a bad citizen as a good one.

In Michigan we have been more fortunate than in many states, because very little of our school program has been established by law. There are many proposals to legislate school programs in each session of the legislature, but they usually come to naught. We do have the requirement of a course in American history or civics in our high schools, but one could hardly escape that anyway. We have a requirement to teach driver training, a "frill" which saves many lives every year. We are further required to teach the dangers of alcohol and to teach children kindness to animals. We have a college requirement of a course in political science for a bachelor's degree, but the legislature repealed the requirement for higher degrees, having belatedly realized that one has to have a bachelor's degree before he can work for a higher one. Curriculum building by our legislature is not very extensive.

Some bizarre proposals have been made. One example will suffice. It is said, though I cannot vouch for the accuracy of this, that in one state it was proposed that *pi,* the ratio between the circumference and diameter of a circle, be made even 3, instead of 3.14159, so that it would be easier to figure. Some harried youths in our mathematics classes would no doubt have hailed this.

We Think Oaths, Pledges, and Other Rituals Make Citizens

We are not only obsessed with the idea of oaths for our boys and girls, but we carry it throughout adult life. We do not seem to realize that a subversive, by the very fact of being one, would be only too happy to take an oath, whereas an honest citizen will always resent the questioning of his integrity.

Oath giving and taking has been revived in recent years. It has a long history. In fact, in the old days of witchcraft and voodooism it was much more suited to man's state of development than it is in this age of alleged science and the use of intelligence in the solution of problems. In the days of Cromwell oaths were required even more than is now the case. It came about that everyone had to administer an oath to everyone else. The idea receded when oath giving and taking became so confusing that nobody could be sure that everybody had been sworn in.

Since it bears directly on the problem of the nurture of our youth, and since it is heavily loaded with oaths and affidavits, this may be as good a place as any to discuss the nurture law passed by Congress in 1958. For at least the last thirty years, perhaps longer, attempts have been made to secure federal aid to education. The idea usually is supported in both party platforms. While these efforts supposedly have the welfare of youth as their base, adults have fought over the money like dogs over a bone, and no bill has ever been passed. Finally, in 1958, somebody hit upon a marvelous idea. Instead of letting people know that an education bill was before them, it could be called a National Defense Act. If people thought that the reason for helping youth was to defend us, that would put an entirely different face on the matter. Since the bill was really not for youth at all, but to defend us, it passed quickly and easily.

This bill, which many believe establishes the pattern for federal aid to education in our time, does not build one building, although our children are packed like sardines in many firetraps. It does not raise the salary of one teacher, although our teachers' salaries are a national disgrace, as nearly everyone admits. It provides no scholarship money, whereby some of our lost youth can choose an education. It creates many presently unestablished programs, arrived at not on account of the needs of youth but because money is available.

It is not my purpose here to discuss this bill in detail, except to note that if we think of the needs of youth and are attempting to improve the nurture of our young, the whole thing is a national disgrace. For a full exposure, I recommend that anyone curious about what is being done with his money read Daniel P. Moynihan on the subject.*

A discussion of this legislation was introduced at this point because of its oath taking features. Mr. Moynihan points out that by the time a student finishes his schooling under this bill, he will owe the government about a year's salary, he will be an engineer, and he will have taken five loyalty oaths and signed five loyalty affidavits. He will have sworn five times (one vaccination and four booster shots, says Mr. Moynihan) that he not only does not belong to any organization advocating the overthrow of the government, but does not *believe* in them. It is the first time that *beliefs* have been made a sign of guilt.

By the time this "educated man" has finished swearing and signing, he will have long since become inured to it, and he, as in the days of Cromwell, will no longer know or care what he swears to. Long since he will have ceased to think about such matters, and his sensibilities necessary to good citizenship will have been damaged. One wonders what the

* Daniel P. Moynihan, "A Second Look at the School Panic" in *The Reporter*, June 11, 1959, Vol. 20, No. 12 p. 14.

Congress was afraid of that they thought could be assuaged by so much swearing.

I do not suppose that anyone should object to the many many instances in which people salute the flag, unless adults think they are making good citizens in this manner. Respect for the flag and love of country have nothing whatever to do with the ritual of facing the flag, holding the right hand over the heart, and mumbling some words which have been made up by someone else. I know a teacher who opens his class by singing three stanzas of the Star Spangled Banner and repeating the prescribed oath of allegiance. His students do not seem to be better citizens than those of other teachers. The whole performance seems to be out of an age gone by. The hand must be on the heart, lest one's patriotism be questioned. But for two or three centuries we have known that the heart is the blood-pump and not the seat of the emotions. We have thought it amusing that the British government used to write the prayers that the people were allowed to pray, but one of the few achievements of the 83rd Congress was to add "under God" to the oath of allegiance. This was soberly debated at length by grown men, because we have some agnostics, atheists, and members of other religions in our land, and we want them to be loyal too.

So tender are our feelings on such matters that some will say I am a traitor, others that I am a Communist. Let me assure them that I am neither of these, not even a heathen. I include these ideas because as long as we think we can make citizens by ritual, it will seem easy and will keep us from facing the real problems of education for citizenship. I would not object to it at all, if we valued it for its real worth and did not expect it to produce results which it clearly cannot and has not done. I think that when anything is reduced to a ritual it tends to defeat the use of intelligence in the solution of human problems. The building of good citizens is too serious an affair to be approached with anything less than the very best thinking and acting of which we are capable.

The six items cited above are ways quite common in our culture by which we hope to produce good citizens. These are what we do *to* youth in our efforts to make them into intelligent, problem-solving members of our democratic society. In all probability, they cause youth to become less sensitive, less capable of fulfilling their proper adult functions.

Perhaps these points could be summed up by merely saying that we do not treat youth as though they were citizens. I imagine there are some adults who do not even know that children are citizens. The United States Constitution, however, is quite specific about this. Article XIV says that "all persons born or naturalized in the United States and of the state wherein they reside, and are entitled to the privileges thereof." It does not say that all those born in the United States will become citizens later on. One does not even have to swear allegiance in order to become a citizen.

The Constitution says that all citizens are created equal, which means that every child is equal before the law, and every child is entitled to the opportunity to reach his potential. It does not mean that all children have equal potential, because the Founding Fathers were thinking in political terms, not biological or psychological terms. The I.Q. had not even been invented, so in those days people did not even have I.Q.'s. Are children and youth in America given equal political and educational opportunity?

The Constitution says that government of citizens shall be by the consent of the governed; that a citizen is considered innocent until he has been proven guilty; and that he shall be secure in his person, papers, and effects. It does not seem necessary to elaborate on the fact that if children are citizens, and if these are their inherent rights, we do not come very close to treating children as citizens.

One of the perquisites of citizenship is the opportunity to vote. This is when the citizen has a chance to have something to say about his government. A newborn babe, although a citizen, obviously cannot vote, and so a time has to be set when the citizen is considered to be literate and comprehending enough to exercise this privilege. From the very beginning, the age for voting has been twenty-one years. This age was established when voting was a sharply restricted privilege. At that time only male land owners were allowed to vote, and it is doubtful that very many people could attain this status under the age of twenty-one. Women in that day never became old enough to vote.

The voting privilege has been broadened a great deal since that time. Men who did not own property were granted this right. Then, in 1918, it was granted that women are also people, perhaps because they spend about eighty per cent of the money. But we still cling to the ancient idea that youth are not people, except in Georgia, and have kept the age for voting at twenty-one.

Whenever an attempt has been made to extend the voting privilege to an additional group, there has been a protest by those who already have the vote that the new group would be too "radical." In the long fight for woman suffrage, the men claimed that the women did not know enough to vote intelligently, and the women claimed that they would clean up "dirty politics," saloons, and vice. Neither side was right. The women turned out to be just as conservative, if not more so, than the men, just as negligent in exercising their new right, and just as susceptible to the blandishments of demagogues.

I bring up this matter of voting because it seems to me that considering the changing times and an improved concept of citizenship, it is time we lowered the voting age. I am not sure how low it should be, but I think we should lower it to eighteen years of age now and continue to study the problem. This is on the assumption that we want to treat youth as though they really are citizens.

The fact is that youth are more competent to vote at eighteen than they are at twenty-one. Schools do try to teach citizenship, although their methods may be criticized. There is no doubt, however, that youth care more and know more about citizenship when they leave school than they do after they have wandered in the no-man's-land of our culture until they are twenty-one. A large number—perhaps as many as forty per cent—leave school at sixteen, and they have five years to wander in the wilderness between childhood and adulthood. By the end of that time they have forgotten whatever learning about citizenship they may have acquired and in many cases have become embittered by the buffeting they have received during the time they have spent outside the fold of society. They have forgotten what the issues were, and of course, those issues no longer exist. Many of them do not show up to vote at all.

The state of Georgia has for a considerable time granted the voting privilege to persons eighteen years of age. If this has caused an upsurge of radicalism in that state, it has been imperceptible from here. Actually, youth are often more conservative than adults. If they are to be treated as citizens, they should have a chance to assume the responsibilities belonging to citizens at an earlier age than is now customary.

Youth will never act as a citizen until he sees himself as citizen. No one ever does anything voluntarily unless he sees it as worthy and worth doing. Our task then is to devise conditions and experiences which will enable a young person to see himself as citizen and hold good citizenship as worth having.

Chapter 9

The School as the Source of Citizens

It has been said earlier that the school is the best place, though not the only one, to concentrate our efforts in the development of citizens. It is the institution where we pool our resources to create a suitable place for youth. We all contribute to its support, since there is no one left any longer who does not pay taxes. We have a right to expect that the school will produce people more able to take their places in a democratic society than if they had not attended school.

Learning to live well, in its broad sense, can best be achieved by living well. The school therefore needs to be a place where it is possible for youth to learn the good life. The school is a society in itself, with most of the problems of any society. It is well suited to practice the ways of democracy. There are many facets to our society—too many for inclusion in any book—so I propose to emphasize ways in which the school may forward the development of competent citizens.

To say that youth need "the good life" is perhaps too general and too easily applauded. I shall attempt to make this more specific in the paragraphs which follow. The specifics are the same as we require for ourselves as we live in our city, state, and nation. They have been set forth many times by the mental hygienists as they tell what anybody needs in order to live a satisfying life.

1) Everyone wants to be *consulted* about what is going on. No one can feel himself to be a citizen in a democracy when all decisions are made in advance by others. Consultation is the first step if one is to become a part of any enterprise. This does not mean that he has to have his own way, but if he never gets any part of his own way, he will not see the program as his. This is true of anybody anywhere. It is also true of youth in school. This means that as a minimum a young person must have a part in planning his program. After he enters the program of which he has had some foreknowledge and to which he has given consent, there must be some teacher-pupil planning. I do not see how anyone can feel himself to be a part of the school society with any less than this. If

he has been consulted, he will have a plan, a path down which his energies may be spent.

2) Everyone must have a *task* which is suitable to him and which he has himself assumed. Something to do which has meaning, and which he sees as forwarding the cause he believes in, is essential to mental health and citizenship. The task does not have to seem significant to anyone but the doer. It has to be seen as important by him. There are many tasks around a school in addition to those provided by the curriculum. We cannot avoid the task problem by giving the student some extra arithmetic problems to solve. There is much work to be done around a school which the students would be only too glad to do, if they thought the school was their school. This is particularly true if we include the grounds and the environment around the school. It might seem that some of these tasks are demeaning in their nature. But a task is never demeaning or ennobling in itself. It is demeaning if it is done for a mean reason; ennobling if the motive is noble. Teachers and youth can be ingenious in finding things for youth to do which will make the school run better. When youth feel part ownership in the school they willingly *do* work to make the school look better. When they do not feel any ownership, but consider that the school belongs to the adults, they *make* work for others, and we have to hire people to clean it up.

3) In order for a task to have meaning we must have *freedom*. All tasks are menial in the absence of freedom. Adults cherish their freedom, and the fact that we do have freedom is one of the things that has made America great. I know that most adults think that youth has too much freedom and that that is what is the matter with them. Young people do break out in rebellion occasionally, and some individuals are in a constant state of rebellion, but youth rebels for the same reason that adults do. That is because they do not have freedom. All rebellions come from too *little* freedom, too *little* choice, not too much.

When I speak of freedom, I mean, of course, freedom within the social scene. I do not mean freedom to do just as one pleases. Nobody has that, unless he lives alone in a wilderness. There would be no reason for citizenship if it were not for other people. Everybody has to take other people into account. But when a task is assumed, choices must be available, and one has to have the right to undertake his task in the way which seems most appropriate to him.

Adult Americans cherish freedom. We sing about it, and on July 4 many orations extoll the glories of freedom, and indeed, it is a wonderful thing. It is wonderful for me, sitting here, to be able to write anything which seems to make sense to me. I may not be able to get it published, but that is entirely an economic matter. The question will be not whether I have a right to say it, but will it sell? And if I win a Nobel prize (a likely example!) I will be allowed to go and pick up the check whether whoever is President by then likes what I have written or not. As an adult, I have many choices open to me. I do not have to write at all; this theme is not due anywhere at any time. I do not have to continue to live in this house or this town.

Though I am a slave to my own purposes, this feeling of freedom is not only precious but essential to me. One of the things that has happened to youth in the last forty years is that his free choices have almost completely disappeared. During the time of compulsory school age he has little choice as to what he will work at. He is handed a program, and although this in itself does not entirely eliminate freedom, the way the program is carried out allows for little or no choice. If he should do any writing, it will not be because he has an urge to express himself, but to have something to hand in. This forced performance may render him forever incapable of expressing himself in writing. When he attains a certain age he can quit school, if his parents are poor. If his parents are in the "upper" economic and social strata, or if they are not but wish they were, he won't even have this choice. He will have to continue in high school and go to college to protect the family name. He may even have to go through the process of trying to become a doctor (a favorite parental ambition) and never escape the program until he suffers the humiliation of being "kicked out." This is a dubious way for a free man to exercise a choice.

If his culture allows him the choice of quitting school, he then has little choice as to what he will do. He cannot "hire out" for farm work. He can no longer go West and stake a claim. He cannot get a respectable job anywhere. He has chosen not to go to school, but there his choices have ended.

We Americans do cherish freedom. But we also fear it. We think it is a fine thing for us, but that it is dangerous for others to have it. We think that if youth has any freedom, he will abuse it. And thus through lack of confidence in youth and faith in others, with its attendant insecurity, authoritarian personalities develop, right under the constitution and under the flag. Lack of faith and confidence does untold harm among adults. At the university where I teach we have an endless number of rules with a large body of clerks checking all day long just to make sure that I (and the likes of me) do not cheat and give away some credits or degrees. I have a feeling, as I fill out blanks in quadruplicate and write memoranda, that if I am not to be trusted I should not have been employed. I also feel that I am fully as trustworthy as the watchdog to whom I write memoranda. But I do not want to single out my university as a sad example. It has as much or more freedom than any other so far as I know. I cite it rather as a symptom of our society and of what can happen to freedom and how little we trust it right under the Stars and Stripes. In case the personal reference above shocks anyone, I might say that it is nothing that I have not told my colleagues and administrators verbally many times.

What the authoritarian mind does to adults is harmful enough, but most adults have built-in defenses which allow them to be people in spite of it. The harm to youth, however, in the violation of freedom is incalculable. They do not have socially acceptable defenses. They have the requirement for freedom built in by the very nature of all purposive organisms, and this drives them so that some form of rebellion is all that is open to them. Freedom within the social scene is, therefore, a requirement for the life good to live.

4) Everyone, in order to become a good citizen, must have *colleagues,* or *peers*. If we look at our massive secondary schools, where sometimes as many as five thousand are packed in one city block, it would seem that the trouble with youth in these schools is that they have too many colleagues. This, however, is a superficial view of what actually goes on. One can be more alone in these schools than if he were out by himself in a wilderness. This is especially true of the "good" boys and girls who "behave themselves." They are expected to stay in their seats with eyes lowered so that they can study, or to pay attention to the teacher. Until recently, we even built schools with windows so high that nobody could see the world outside. Students aren't permitted to help one another. They often have to sign oaths that they have "neither given or received help." Middle-aged teachers in our Education Workshop* have testified that this is the first time they have ever become acquainted with a classmate. I think many people would be surprised to know how many young people are desperately lonely in the midst of thousands.

When I say a young person must have colleagues, I do not mean that he must be packed in the same can with them. I mean that he must have them as working peers. This gives him an opportunity to develop his cortex, which can only be developed through social contact and interchange. It enables him to form friendships which assuage the

* For a more complete description of this workshop see Earl C. Kelley, *The Workshop Way of Learning* (New York: Harper & Brothers, 1951).

loneliness of the human spirit. It also gives him an opportunity to develop his potential for leadership, and to lead when his unique talents are in demand. A certain amount of leadership is a requirement for good citizenship, but it cannot develop in the absence of other people. Surely having others in a serious, working relationship is a requirement for the life good to live.

Chapter 10

The School Can Teach Citizenship

If youth living in towns and cities are to have the minimum requirements for mental health; if they are to lead the life good to live, most of these requirements will have to be met by the school. Of course, a loving, cooperative home will help a great deal, and if it is good enough, it may supply all that is needed. But our homes in general are not that good; there appears to be little chance that they will be. As has been pointed out, there is not room enough in and around most city homes, nor is there likely to be. Difficult as it is, it seems that our best chance is to change the school, to make it a real youth institution. Changing the school is almost as difficult as changing the home, but at least the adults in the school are paid by the public, and so if the public wants a place that is good for nurturing its young, it has the right to ask for it. This will not change teachers and administrators into loving people, but we can at least start in that direction. We can only make parents more loving people by raising them in that atmosphere when they are young.

This would be the most important thing that young people could learn if it could be done. They would then become parents who would naturally know how to establish a cooperative, love-centered home. Hostility feeds on itself, and perpetuates itself. So our avenue to the home is through the young, many of whom will be parents soon after they leave school. Indeed, it is the one thing that we know most of them will do. It is the only career we can predict with a high degree of probability.

As it is now, although we know these high school youth will very soon be fathers and mothers, we are so busy teaching them such matters as adverbial clauses and mathematical (not baby) formulas, that we have no time to teach them attitudes necessary in a closely knit world. When a girl has left school, either via carnations or the back door, marries and becomes pregnant, the adult education people become excited because she does not know how to take care of her infant even physically, not to mention the necessary emotional or psychological care. So the adult education forces try to entice her back to night class, although by this time she does not feel very good.

It is, of course, true that some effort has been made in so-called home economics classes to give her some of the minimal facts of life, but these often refer only to the physical aspects of infant care. And these courses, skimpy as they are, do not receive the respect of most teachers or the public. I suspect they are what is meant by "frills," perhaps because they might be useful and enjoyable. The students might like these classes and develop friendly attitudes toward the world and its people. They might transmit these feelings, instead of hostility, to their young. In the development of citizens, love of people is not a frill, but an absolute necessity.

Student Participation in School Government

In a large school, where there are likely to be many lost and lonely ones, I believe that one of the best ways to assure that there will be no forgotten ones is through a proper system of student participation in school government. Of course, there is nothing better than a loving relationship between teacher and youth. But that is likely to be haphazard and to leave out too many. Student participation in school government is a way by which every person may be made to feel that he belongs to the school and the school in part belongs to him. It is ideal for the teaching of active citizenship, because the school does operate, and it is a society in itself. It has to be organized in such a way that the least of them feels that he is a member of that society and that he does have a citizen's rights and responsibilities.

Unfortunately, most of the systems of student participation in government do not educate for citizenship because they are really adult shams. They are operated to pretend or to give lip service to democratic living. But they do not provide for any real participation nor do they involve the vast majority of the student body. Joe Doakes in the back seat, of whom there are many and whom we will later have to ask to vote for school bonds, does not know who is on the council or what it does, and he couldn't care less. He probably did have a chance to vote, unless he had been disfranchised because of low grades, but he did not know any of the candidates or expect the winners to affect his life in any way.

The adults in the school usually do such a careful job of blocking freedom that before the students are involved at all everything is safe. All risks have been fended. The candidates for office are from among the "nice" young people, and by setting up rules for candidacy they have really been picked by the teachers. This kind of "student government" is not always the case, of course. It is not the kind I am recommending as having a bearing on education for citizenship.

In the next pages I will describe my own experience in operating a system of student participation in school government. I hope the reader will not be repelled by too much reference to self. After all, though, I doubt that there is any better place for one to get material for writing than from experience. Also, I do not want to recommend too many things which I have not done, and which can, therefore, be dismissed as theoretical. The fact is that I probably would not be writing this book except that I have learned for myself that young people want a good society and will help build one. This is a great discovery.

But first I must tell you about the school where this experience took place, for it was no ordinary school—no ordinary student body. This was the Milwaukee Vocational School, which during the 1930's was one of the brightest spots in American education. There were more good spots in education in that decade than there have been since, or so it seems to me. We have regressed in our concern for youth and in providing places for them to grow.

In Wisconsin, the law requires young people to attend school until they are either graduated from high school or have reached their eighteenth birthday. They do not have to go to the regular school, but are provided with a vocational school which they may attend. Milwaukee, being the largest city in the state, had the largest vocational school. This school was centrally located downtown, was seven stories high and filled a city block. It was a new school at that time, having been built in 1928. The attendance law had been passed in 1912, but a suitable place for the youth who could not or would not take the regular high school curriculum came much later.

The law stated that youth could hold jobs, provided that they secured permits. In that case they attended school only one day a week. Some students came full time; some came a half day each day; and some only one day a week. There were many shops for teaching trades, as many as sixty different trades for boys and a large number for girls. There were academic classrooms, where students were taught, broadly speaking, English, mathematics and social studies. Mathematics, however, was for the most part taught in the shops as the need arose.

This school when I was employed had 13,500 young people attending the day school and about 9,000 adults in the evening school, so that about 22,000 individuals came to the school for longer or shorter periods every week. In head count it was larger than most of our large universities at that time.

The school was the realization of the dream of Robert L. Cooley. Here was one of the great educators of all time, although many readers will never have heard of him. That is because he never wrote anything, and the character of the school has now been changed. It is most important that such people make records, because the world moves on and we are mortal. Writing is time-binding; it takes a picture, so to speak, to show the scene at any particular time.

Dr. Cooley was principal of an elementary school in Milwaukee in 1912 when the law establishing the vocational school and requiring attendance was passed. He had nothing to do, I believe, with the passage of the law; but he was named director of vocational education for Milwaukee and thenceforth became the champion of the law and of the youth whom it affected. He did the political work to improve the law and to get adequate financial backing. He insisted that nothing but the best was good enough for those he referred to as the "educationally disinherited." He had wit so sharp that he often routed opposition with a phrase. It is probable that the powers in the city never intended to build that school. Some said that nobody could learn anything in just one day a week, to which he replied, "You probably send your children to Sunday school for one hour a week, don't you?" Then he would say, "It is the quality of an experience that matters, not its duration."

The law provided for a separate board of education for vocational schools. The board was made up of two representatives of employers, two from labor, and the superintendent of schools, who was expected to mediate points of view between these two powerful forces. The law was continually under attack by educators all over the country who contended that two boards of education in a community were one, at least, too many, and that the total educational effort in the community should be under one board. Dr. Cooley's rejoinder was that you don't scramble your eggs in order to see each one better. I must say that I do not know a large community outside Wisconsin which has provided anything comparable to what was provided under the two boards.

I have not forgotten my initial interview with Dr. Cooley. They were having much trouble with the behavior of their students, and they wanted somebody to "clean up the discipline." He talked to me for two hours, during which time I said nothing. He asked me no questions about myself. He was too full of his school. Then he called in Mr. Robert Otis, who kept track of signed agreements and money matters, and told him that he had had a fine talk with me and believed that I was just the man they wanted. Since I was unemployed and the day of the interview was Black Tuesday, I was in no mood to debate and so was hired.

I wish I had a tape recording of the interview. There were many educational gems. I remember, however, that he told me that it is not a boy or girl who comes to school but a whole situation. His parents, his home, his strengths, weaknesses, and fears all come with him. He also said that day, "We have no quarrel with the child's antecedents." In other words, we do not care what his race or creed is, how much the child knows or does not know; we are not at war with him for his accident of birth, where he has been or what he has done. We accept him as a person, and if we judge, it will be on the basis of present performance. Nowadays, it seems to me, we spend a good deal of time and energy quarreling with the child's antecedents.

One remarkable feature of this school was that there were no grades, no graduation, no transfer of credits. The school was not preparatory to any other school. There was no separation of the sheep from the goats. Nobody ever got anything from the school except what he learned. We had students who did not do very well, but they just profited less from their time than the others. We had no failures in the sense that we named them as such. We did not need any, because we did not have any promotions. Of course, we gave better recommendations to employers for those who did well than for those who did not. This is in the nature of life itself. It is surprising how many of the vexations of teaching are removed when we free ourselves from these extrinsic rewards and punishments. If education is growth, it is hard to see how one can flunk a year's growth, or, if he grows badly, how he can recover the time he has wasted.

To be sure, we had the advantage that our students, except in rare instances achieved by entrance examinations, were not going to any other school later, because they did not have high school diplomas. We have, however, many large high schools today whose students are not going on. I know a large high school which issues less than five transcripts a year, but they still maintain a college preparatory program and act as though they were teaching not for now, but for some mythical "other school."

This school had a small high school division, but it was for adults only, so that an adult who had missed his chance to graduate from high school could still do so. Persons under eighteen were not permitted to enroll in this division, because the regular high schools of the city were available to them. I believe that the high school division never exceeded one hundred people while I was there. It was a very good opportunity for a few adults.

The student body was a wonderful sight to behold. It was the American melting pot at its best. Dr. Cooley used to say that we had the output and the put-out of the public schools. They were all nationalities, all colors, all creeds. While they came mostly from the lower economic and cultural strata of society, they were by no means stupid. Some had come to us because the academic curricula of the high schools were unsuited to them. Some came because they refused to submit to the high school program. About seventy-five came each year because they had been expelled from high school. We had a good many who had been pegged as delinquent in one way or another. Some were mentally ill, having been too badly damaged by the lives they had been forced to live to take their places in regular schools. Many were there only because the law required them to be, although a considerable number of these came to like what they were learning and stayed on after they had met the legal requirements. My over-all impression is and was that while we had many problems, they were on the whole a wonderful collection of young people. Not wanting to finish high school can happen to some very fine people.

While we had a few adults taking courses, the great majority of the students were between the ages of 14 and 18. To be admitted one had to finish the eighth grade or have spent nine years trying to. If he was sixteen and still had not finished the eighth grade, we would accept him.

Now I want to show how all this relates to education for citizenship. As I have said, I was employed in the fall of 1929 to "clean up the discipline." And, indeed, the relationships between youth and age at that time in this school were pretty bad. By the very nature of the school we had many problems, and the only thing the adults seemed able to think to do was to fight back. To walk down the hall during the passing of classes was an adventure in itself. One needed to be pretty shifty on his feet, and the ability to put out an elbow at the right time was a valuable asset.

The teachers' heads were bloody but not unbowed. When I say bloody, it is not entirely a figure of speech. Fist fights between teachers and youth in the halls were not uncommon. I well remember that during my first week there the teacher of the tin shop and a large seventeen year old had come to grips in the shop. They had clinched and gone over on the floor and rolled over and over. Now the tin shop floor had many little cuttings of metal on it, and every time they rolled over the tin scraps did their work impartially on youth and age alike. When they got to my office (an odd place to go) they were, like Caesar, bleeding from all of their veins. Neither was hurt much, but a bloodier sight I have never seen. I do not remember what I did or said, only the sight, but what I said must have been highly anti-climactic.

I did not have the slightest idea what to do about the task I had so blithely accepted. I had been a high school science teacher in a school where we had no problems. But in the early days of the job I had some good luck which enhanced my reputation, and lasted me until I could figure out something intelligent to do.

For example, on the morning of my third day a boy came to me and told me that he had lost twenty dollars, an enormous sum for those hard times.

"How did you come to have so much money?" I asked.

"My ma gave it to me to pay the taxes."

"What pocket did you have it in?"

"I had it in my hip pocket."

"Anything else in the pocket?"

"Yes," he said. "My handkerchief was in it."

"Have you used your handkerchief this morning?"

"Yes, when I was in the lavatory."

"Was there anyone else in the lavatory at that time?"

"Yes, Joe——— was in there."

There were thousands of students in the school at the time, but I looked up Joe's program and found that he was in a class on the sixth floor. I went up to the class and asked to see him. When he came out into the hall, I said, "Joe, I've come for that twenty dollars." He reached in his pocket and handed it to me! And so the word spread that they had a new man in the office who could see in one's pocket from the second to the sixth floor.

There were many dramatic scenes—some frightening, some pathetic, some humorous. And sometimes these were all mixed in one incident. While I was still in my first week on the job, Angelo was brought to me because he had attacked his teacher with a sturdy piece of scrap iron with the vowed intention of murdering him. As we sat in my office his face was a picture of defiant rebellion. I started to say something, and he looked bored, as much to say "Well, here we go! Another sermon on right and wrong!" But before I could complete the first sentence, he interrupted me saying, "Ach! Don't worry! I ain't gonna kill him. He ain't worth it!"

One time during the first few weeks someone brought a note to my office telling me that Mr.——— had sent for me to come to his room because he had told Ed——— to leave the room but Ed had refused to do so, and the teacher wanted me to do something about it. This was a poser. What to do? Rather unhappily I went to the room, wishing I were somewhere else. I did not have to have Ed pointed out to me. There he sat, about 190 pounds of him, gripping his desk with both hands and glaring defiance. I went up to him and said very quietly, "Are you Ed———?" He nodded. Then in the same low voice I said, "I am Mr. Kelley from the office. Come with me." He got up and came with me! I have never had to answer the question as to what I would have done if he hadn't.

Big Tony lived in the third ward, which was the Italian section of town. He had had a good deal of trouble so that he and I had seen each other a good deal. One day he came into my office and said he wanted to ask me a question. Upon being encouraged, he asked me if he could be my body-guard. I said, "Why Tony, this is a very fine offer, but I don't need a body-guard." "Oh yes, you do!" said Tony. I declined his offer, but it was a bit unsettling because I couldn't entirely dismiss the idea that Tony might know something that I didn't.

And I must tell about Stanley. Stanley was a sort of confirmed juvenile delinquent, frequently getting into trouble with the law in one way or another, although not particularly troublesome in school. But he and I had a good many sessions. During one of these, he told me that he had an uncle in Rockford, Illinois, who was a tailor and that his uncle had told him that when he became eighteen, the uncle would take him into his business. I suggested that he go into our tailoring shop so that he would already know something about the trade when he got to Rockford. This seemed neat—a trade, a purpose, and a chance to get him out of the state. So it was agreed, and all seemed to go well for a time.

The next time I saw Stanley I noted that he was not in the tailoring shop but had transferred to another trade. I asked why he had done this and how his uncle would feel about it. He said in an expressionless voice, "I ain't going to Rockford to work for my uncle."

"You're not! Why not?"

Without batting an eyelash and without any expression, he said, "Because he is gonna be hung."

I was talking to Tito one day because he seemed, though a lad of good will, to have trouble getting to school when he was supposed to. He told me that his father had died recently and that he had had a good many things to do. I asked him to tell me more about his father and what caused his death. He said that he and his father had made a living by trucking produce from Chicago to Milwaukee and that they often made the trip back in the early hours before dawn. One night Tito was driving the truck and his "pa" was sitting beside him. It was a very warm night, so his pa's shirt was open, and he had a large growth of hair on his chest. His pa was smoking, and a spark flew from his cigarette, setting the hair on his chest on fire. Tito said, "I saw the blaze, and I tried to put my pa out, and I ran off the road and hit a tree, and my pa died." I thought that missing a few days of school was a rather trivial matter under such circumstances.

These anecdotes are only a few that have stayed in my memory for upward of thirty years. They have never been recorded before, and if I had been a systematic person and had kept good records of this rare adventure, I could write a whole book of them. But then, if I had been such a person, perhaps I would not have had the adventure.

My problem, as can readily be seen, was one in education for citizenship. But I had no idea how to do it. The best I could think of in the beginning was to sit in my office and talk to people who were in trouble. Mostly these were people who had been sent to me by teachers because the teachers had been annoyed by them in one way or another. Some, of course, were very serious problems. The teachers wanted evidence that the youth had been "counseled." Sometimes I wished I had a branding iron to show the teachers that I had done my work. For often the counselled ones behaved even worse when they got back to class, for reasons which now seem easy to understand.

At any rate, since none of us knew anything better to do, I sat in my office from November to the following June and talked to boys who either had serious problems or had annoyed their teachers or both. Sometimes there were as many as twenty boys sitting outside my office waiting to come in and receive "the word." The conversation, much boiled down, would go something like this:

"Now, Joe, you know better than to do what you did, don't you?"

"Yes sir, I know better."

"Then you won't do it any more, will you?"

"No, sir, I won't do it any more."

Then he would go back to class and do it again.

One incident which was repeated frequently tended to jangle my nerves. Joe would come into the office, the door would be closed so that we were alone. I would say, "Joe, Mr.——— says that you have done so and so."

Joe would look surprised and say, "Who, me?"

It began to occur to me after a few months that I was engaged in a losing battle, that I was not "cleaning up the discipline" as I had been employed to do. The incidents of conflict were no fewer than they had been, and I was only serving as a buffer between the teachers and the boys. That was a fine case of being "in the middle." I realized by June that something had to be invented by September, because what I had been doing was wrong in principle.

I believe that the "desk" or "office" guidance counselor will always be in that spot. As long as he stays in his office he will never be able to do more than to sweep up the dirt that other people make. The trouble, except in the case of a few sick people, is being made by the nature of the program and the people who operate it. No matter how good the counselor is at cleaning up other people's dirt, they will always be able to make it faster than he can clean it up. So, even if he is effective, which is seldom the case, he will always be behind. His only alternative is to do something to affect what is going on throughout the school so that the trouble that is made will be reduced and less cleaning up will be needed. It is a shame to point out anything so obvious, and I would not stoop so low if it were not for what I know many counselors are still doing, but trouble which never starts does not have to be dealt with, and no "dealing with it" is as good as though it never had occurred.

Many a counselor seems to think that the program of the school—what is going on all around him—is really none of his business, since his job is to counsel. He enjoys having more status than teachers do, that he is not "just a teacher." And so, by occupying a swivel chair in an office and by flaunting his status, he widens the gulf between himself and the teachers and students. In the degree that this gulf exists, he renders himself less able to be useful in the school; the wider the separation, the less his usefulness becomes.

The guidance worker needs, I believe, to realize that program, curriculum, and teacher attitudes toward the young are his business and that here is the place where he can best fulfill his own mission. So far as actual guidance of youth is concerned he should realize that it can best be done by the adult who knows the youth best and sees him most often—the teacher. I think it would be a good thing if the counselor saw himself as supervisor of human relations in the school. The word "supervisor" has long since been discredited, but we still have supervisors for each subject with human relations neglected and deteriorating. Teacher attitudes toward youth are probably the most important factor in any school, because attitude controls behavior, and the behavior of the teacher toward the student builds him or diminishes him. If the student is diminished, it may bring forth aggressive behavior, causing a rift which the counselor is expected to mend. In most cases, however, the counselor cannot do this.

Pondering all this, it seemed to me that while we had a splendid school from a physical standpoint, and we had a fine human grist, the adults and the students in the school were actually working against each other instead of with each other. Having had time to gain some appreciation of the real quality of the young people, it seemed that it was not necessary to work against them, and if we could switch and start pulling in the same direction instead of opposite directions, we could live fruitfully together in peace.

What we needed was a spirit of cooperation between adults and youth. But no one can be expected to cooperate in the absence of consultation. If a person never has a chance to express an opinion on what is going on or what might be, he cannot see that there is anything to cooperate about. We had to invent a way by which even the least of them would feel that he was a part of the enterprise and that in some measure what he thought was important. To do this, we created a large and comprehensive system of student participation in school government.

One cannot start a cooperative operation by decree. It was necessary to get as many teachers persuaded as possible. This was done by many meetings with teachers in the large groups, in small groups, and singly. Casual visits with teachers in the halls, in the lunch room, and in their classes went on for some time. I was sure that we had to have the honest cooperation of a large majority of the teachers if we were to succeed. These teachers were not, for the most part, academically hardened authoritarians. One of the great obstacles to cooperation in many high schools is that there are too many teachers who will say that they are going to run their classes as they please without any nonsense from anybody.

We did not, however, have very many such people. Most of them were thoroughly tired of conflict and were willing to "try anything once." Many of them already believed in the ideas I was proposing and helped to persuade others. I think this particular group of teachers was more favorably inclined toward cooperation than most senior high school faculties would be. They were also more battered.

After it seemed that every teacher knew and understood what we were going to try to do, we then began to work with the students. We did our best through many avenues to let the students know what we were thinking and to ask them whether or not they would like to enter into cooperative operation of the school. Every student attended assembly once a week, so our huge auditorium was full to the roof five times a week.

We made speeches in the assembly. We talked with almost any group we could find. The teachers explained in classrooms. Our biggest problem was to convince our students that we would not double-cross them. (This is still my biggest job as I work with adult graduate students who are already teachers. This is a good time to stop and reflect on what we teachers and professors have done to ourselves that we are no longer believed.)

It would be unreasonable to say that all our students knew and understood what we were proposing. We did what we could to consult as many as possible, and the great majority of those consulted thought they would like to try it. Some of these had been booted out of high school, some had records of delinquency, but most of them were just regular nice people who had chosen our school because they thought they would like it better.

There were some things we knew in advance that we wanted to achieve.

1) We wanted everybody under the roof of the school to be included. It was not a student council we were proposing, because if it was to succeed, everybody—the administrators, the teachers, the maintenance people—all must be part of it. And so we called it the "School Council," not the student council. We wanted everybody who could contribute to the success of our undertaking to have a feeling of partnership in it.

2) We wanted everybody to have a chance to discuss. A feeling of partnership can only come when the person can say what he thinks.

3) We wanted everybody to have frequent opportunities to propose changes—what he thought would be improvements—in any feature of the school. He had to get the consent of most of his peers, just as I would have to do if I wanted a change in the laws of Michigan, but it was essential that he have the opportunity to try.

4) We wanted everyone who came to the school to have something to do to make the school operate better every time he came. This ideal was never fully achieved, but ingenious teachers and class officers performed miracles in order to reach achievement.

5) We wanted the adults in the school to have faith in the general rightness and goodness of youth—to feel that youth can be trusted—that they do not have to be viewed with suspicion and fear. We wanted the adults to behave in such a way that youth would view them as people of integrity, and that youth would know that we would live up to any agreements we made.

6) We thought the School Council should be over all of the other activities of the school. In adult society the government is over everything, as it should be. The School Council must not be another extra-

curricular activity, like the hobby club, for example. Of course, such clubs could be formed without the consent of the School Council, just as I can organize a bridge club if I want to. It is none of the state's business unless the club starts some illegal activity.

How It Worked

We worked toward these objectives a little at a time with as much mutual consent as we could get. In order that everyone might belong to a council group, we established a time of day which we called council time, and every shop and class in the school stopped at that time and first held an election and later held council meetings which were legislative in nature. These "council times" usually occurred once a month. It was quite a sight to see the machine shop or the foundry shut down when council time arrived, have the boys all go to their seats and conduct a council meeting with the teacher, often a tradesman rather than a certified teacher, helping.

Each group, wherever it was, started by electing a class president and secretary. The secretary, along with the usual secretarial duties, acted as alternate president when the latter was absent. Each group, then, had its own officers, and nobody had had to vote for anybody he did not know. All of the business the individual transacted in a governmental way was done with his own classmates.

We did not start out by writing a constitution. We did not even know in detail what we were going to do, except that whatever it was, it would be in consultation with others. If the need arose for a constitution as an organization developed, then it would be a matter of putting in writing the things that had already been going on. Our constitution was our good faith, which is liberating. Most of the constitutions which high school student governments have are a set of limitations to hedge against this, that, or the other. Their effect is to confine, rather than to liberate.

To give some idea of the size of the undertaking, we had eight hundred class officers after the first election. They were not all in school at any one time, so that whatever we tried to do with them had to be done several times in order to include everyone. We had more class officers than most high schools have in their total enrollment.

We realized that in addition to the monthly class council meetings, we needed an organization through which the decisions reached could be channeled. We also knew that not too many people could confer together so that mass meetings of large numbers of class officers would not be valuable. So we grouped the eight hundred into groups of ten to fifteen, being governed by the times the officers were in school. Each one of these groups chose a president and a secretary, and these in turn were grouped. Finally there were only about twelve left, each one having been chosen three times. This group of about a dozen we called the School Council, and they in turn chose officers, so that we had one person who was president of the whole School Council, and one who was secretary.

It probably would have been a good idea to have the class councils meet oftener than once a month, but it took a month to operate the machinery so that resolutions passed by the class could be processed by the time another batch started. The School Council had to meet at night because not all of them were in school at any one time. It met every Monday night for years.

Let us now see how an idea for improving the school starts and what happens to it. During a regular monthly class council meeting, Joe Doakes rises and moves, for example, that stairway traffic be made one-way. I do not recall that this ever occurred, but it will serve as a good example. If it is seconded, the class debates its merits and difficulties. The class may vote against it, and if that occurs, the matter has ended. Joe did not get the support of his own class. But the class may approve it. If so, it is copied on what we called a resolution blank, printed for the purpose. The blank is signed by Joe as the originator and by his class president.

Then the president of the class must take the resolution to his "presidents" group and present it. He does not have to argue for it and may even oppose it. This group may reject the idea in which case it is returned to Joe with the objections raised by the group written on the blank. If this group passes it, then it is copied onto another resolutions blank of another color, the two are clipped together, and the president of this group takes it to his next group. It is true that one blank could have served for all, but we thought the different colored blanks added importance to the government, and supplying them gave the boys in the print shop a chance to take part.

If a resolution survived three groups, it came to the School Council. An idea had to be pretty good to get this far, but enough of them did so that we usually had a sizable backlog of resolutions to deal with. If a resolution was passed by the top council, it was signed by the president and by me as faculty representative and then sent to the principal. The principal had agreed that such an idea would either be put into practice, or he would explain in writing why it could not be. For example, some of the ideas called for funds which were not available or were not workable for many reasons.

The principal during this time was William F. Rasche, and one reason our undertaking worked is that he always carried out his agreements meticulously. He put many of the ideas into operation; those he could not, he wrote a full explanation of the problem and the resolution with the explanation on it was returned, not to me or the president of the council, but to Joe Doakes himself. Indeed, it is not possible to operate a cooperative student participation in school government unless the top administration acts in good faith. Perhaps you wouldn't believe it, but this they do not always do.

It will be seen that we never promised the students that we would do whatever they suggested. Nor did we tell them that certain matters were all right for them to discuss and that other matters were none of their business. Everything about the school was open to discussion and criticism. The administrators promised that they would do their best to cooperate. As long as adults work in good faith and openly with the students, youth will be satisfied. When the principal had to reject an idea it was not called a veto. He did not veto an idea, but explained why he could not do it. There is a difference.

So Joe Doakes in the back seat had his chance at least once a month. He might be the originator of a new rule or procedure. Failing that, he got an explanation either from the principal or from someone on the way up. In addition to the many chances to be of help in his own class, he could possibly influence the whole school.

Not every suggestion for improvement had to originate in the class council. Anyone who was a member of any of the presidents' councils could present a new idea. Some of them started in the evening meetings of the top council. In other words, anybody who was in any council meeting could present a proposal.

The adults in the school often presented matters for general discussion. This was usually done by sending mimeographed material to the class council meetings asking that the students talk it over and legislate concerning it if they wanted to. One example that I recall occurred when we were vexed by complaints of citizens because our students misbehaved on the street cars. We were not sure that this was so, since many people had the habit of blaming everything on the vocational school boys. They "helped" us by referring to our school as "Bum's College." We had no need, however, to worry about guilt. We presented the problem to the class councils in one of their regular monthly meetings. It is hard to say whether or not this settled the matter, but many good discussions were held on the effects of bad citizenship outside of the school, and it seemed to us that the complaints were greatly reduced.

Once in a great while we used the public address system, but we tried to avoid doing this unless some kind of emergency arose.

We did everything we could to make being an officer important, so that those who were elected, as well as those who were not, considered it an honor. A badge was issued to each officer showing what office he had been elected to. This made it possible for any officer to be identified in the halls, assemblies, or wherever he went. These badges were almost always worn with pride.

We furnished a good place for the council meetings to be held. One day shortly after the first elections, Dr. Cooley asked me how things were going. I said I thought they were going as well as could be expected.

"What do you need?" he asked.

"Well, we need a decent place to meet. At present we're using a room in the basement with almost no outside light, and the reason we're using it is that nobody else wants it. It is hard to dignify government, to make the students believe that we really think the council is important, in such a place."

"Let me know what you want," he said.

I picked out two classrooms on the south side of the building on the second floor. We took out the partition between them and made a council room, a waiting room, and two offices, one for Mrs. Belding* and one for myself. The whole interior was panelled in solid black walnut. The upper walls were finished in ornamental plaster; the ceiling was sound proofed; the floors were of rubber tile.

At one end of the room there was a platform with a beautiful walnut desk and a railing somewhat like a courtroom, although it was not meant for a court. For the council members there were individual walnut desks and upholstered walnut chairs. Our waiting room where our secretary sat and our offices were furnished in the same way.

When students came into this room they felt its dignity, and they could see that we thought the government of the school was important. Since all meetings above the class councils were held in this room, it was in use most of the time, and many different students got a chance to use it. During the seven years that I know about not a single mark or scratch was made on any of the desks.

This room cost about $11,000. It was, I am sure, more elaborate than necessary. Those were depression dollars and might be equivalent to about thirty thousand now. But the youth whose spirits were lifted were depression youth too, and their need for beauty was very great.

* Mrs. Cora Belding was dean of women, and participated whole-heartedly in the enterprise.

Milwaukee County had just finished a $6 million courthouse complete with pillars, within sight of the council room. One day I heard an alderman who was being shown the building say to Dr. Cooley that the room looked pretty expensive.

"Yes," said Dr. Cooley. "This room cost eleven thousand dollars. But we thought that if the people could spend six millions for a Taj Mahal to send people to jail, we could afford eleven thousand to keep them out."

I have gone into some detail here because I believe that students are not likely to take student participation in government seriously unless we do. I do not think a school needs to spend as much as we did, but I do believe that the council must have a good place to meet; otherwise we run the risk of giving the impression that we consider other activities more important than government.

Our success far exceeded our expectations. I learned then and have often had it confirmed that when we depend upon people to control themselves, either youth or adults, they will do more and better than any authoritarian can make them do. We took all of the monitors out of the halls on the theory that if one is to learn self-control, he has to do it without anybody watching him. We had no teachers on "hall duty." Of course, there were teachers and student officers all around, but they were going about their business. We had no teachers on guard in the cafeteria. We had an assembly every morning with about 2,200 young people present (one assembly per week per person) without an adult in the room except the one responsible for the program. The halls, though not quiet, were as orderly as I have ever seen, and one no longer had to defend himself in going from one classroom to another.

Many of the evidences of youth's hostility toward adults were lessened. The paper thrown on the hall floors, often right beside a container, practically disappeared. It was not uncommon to see a student pick up a wad of paper thrown by someone else. The boys' lavatories (I'm not sure about the girls'), so often places where youth resentment is vented with paper all over the floor and obscenity on the walls, became as clean as such places could be expected to be. (Of course, the idea of ever having such places in a school is a mistake—an invitation to trouble. If I had my way, no school would ever build a general lavatory again. There could be a small washroom for each two classrooms, which both boys and girls would use just as brothers and sisters do at home. We would thus do away with all of the bickering that goes on about who can go to the lavatory and when. It is true that young people ask to go to the lavatory to escape from the classroom. They stay as long as they dare, and hanging around in such a place calls out the worst impulses. If they stay too long, the teacher has to have another quarrel with them about that. Today some of the new schools have abolished the general lavatory.)

Operating school dances became a function of the School Council. I want to make clear that running a dance or raising money is not the primary function of a school council. Too often that is all they do. But school dances had been quite a problem in this school, and for several years none had been held, because they had had trouble with strangers drifting in and had also had some trouble about drinking. Previous to my arrival, a large, well-built staff member had said he would run the dance and that he was prepared to take all comers. This resulted in his being badly beaten and thrown out into the street. The dance became a riot and had to be quelled and dispersed by the police. That ended school dances for several years.

This illustrates the point that we adults cannot win by fighting. There are too many youth. Indeed, we cannot operate a school at all except at the sufferance of the student body. The teacher may not get thrown out bodily, but he could never win in a fair fight.

It will be seen why it was that we approached the first school dance conducted by the School Council with considerable concern. I attended it with the idea of running if a fight started. I believe I was the only faculty member present except Gerald M. Van Pool who helped me with the council continuously. Although he was not paid extra for it, he came to nearly all of our night functions and council meetings because he liked young people. Incidentally, he succeeded me when I left and later became Assistant Secretary of the National Association of Secondary Principals, an affiliate of the National Education Association. Much credit is due him for the success of the whole enterprise.

The dance, and succeeding ones, were fine affairs. Everybody had a good time, the officers were alert so that outsiders did not intrude. It takes youth to know how to deal with such things.

As I have said, the cooperative enterprise succeeded far beyond our dreams. I am afraid that I had grave doubts about it when we started and was grasping at straws in search of a solution to my problem. I could see, however, that it would be foolish to enter into it in a half-hearted way, and I really meant it when I offered sincere cooperation. The magnificent results revealed some very important things to me about youth and about people.

I do not want to give the impression that we had no problems left. There was, however, a marked reduction in the minor complaints, such as whispering, what some teachers call impudence, truancy and tardiness. We had with us, of course, some people who had been so badly damaged that they were beyond the reach of the cooperative process. In working with such individuals, I had much contact with the social agencies, social workers, and psychiatrists. Dr. R. A. Jefferson, a psychiatrist in private practice, gave much free time to my damaged ones, often with excellent results. We could have kept a fulltime school psychiatrist busy if we had had one.

I had much help from the juvenile court and its probation officers. John J. Kenney, who later became Judge of the Juvenile Court, was chief probation officer, and he was always helpful. Having the support of the juvenile court was a great boon. If a boy was so damaged that we could not deal with him, we could always take him to the court building, and the probation officer for the territory where he lived invariably did what he could to help.

Often I had occasion to appear in criminal court. Once I got ordered out of a federal judge's chambers because I came to tell him about a boy who was to appear before him for driving a stolen car across a state line. He said I was trying to prejudice him before the trial. Maybe so.

The outstanding features of this system of student participation were:

1) Everyone was a member and was made to feel so at least once a month. He was given the opportunity to vote for someone in his own class whom he knew. He got frequent opportunities to express his opinion. In addition, he got many chances between monthly meetings to serve his class and his school.

2) Nobody was disfranchised or denied the right to hold office. In many schools adult restrictions are put on those who have not met certain adult standards. The result of this is that those who have been doing poorly because they do not feel involved become more isolated and do worse. Sometimes the argument is advanced that if they are behind in their work, they need to devote more time to it. It is not lack of time, as a rule, which causes youth to do little in school. Giving more time is just the opposite of what is needed. Being barred from the full requisites of citizenship is harmful rather than helpful. The students themselves are the best judges as to who their leaders really are, and it is usually somebody we adults would not pick. Once a boy with a considerable record of delinquency was elected president of the School Council. He was an able one, and so far as I know, never had any more trouble. He would have been the last one the adults, including myself, would have picked. Many so-called "problem" boys and girls improved

with responsibility, did well the jobs to which they were elected, and improved their school work. This did not always occur, but in the main it was true.

3) There were no forbidden subjects for discussion, no drawing of lines of authority. When one enters into an enterprise which is truly cooperative in spirit, he does not say "I will cooperate if you only talk about certain matters." In cooperation there are no jurisdictional boundaries. Of course, there were some things we could not do, for reasons apparent to all, and we adults never promised we would do anything we were asked to do. That would be one-sided cooperation, which is a contradiction in terms. But we said we would try. As soon as one draws a jurisdictional line, with one group having control on one side of the line and another on the other, something arises which both sides think belongs to them. A good deal of the energy on both sides is then spent in bickering. Cooperation ceases when lines are drawn and sides are taken. Why should not anything in the operation of a school be talked about by anybody concerned?

4) The adults never went back on their cooperative agreements. It may come as a surprise to some to learn that teachers and principals do often make agreements which are then not carried out. Sometimes they have to back out because they should never have made such promises, and when the time comes they find they have promised something which they cannot do. This results in all adults being held in suspicion. In my own present classes, made up of in-service teachers and administrators, the students watch all semester for the expected double-cross. If a youth thinks you are going to double-cross him, it is not possible for him to enter wholeheartedly into a cooperative agreement. Since teachers and other adults are held in suspicion from the beginning confidence can only come through good living. Do not promise what you may not be able to perform; if you promise, then do it.

Many more points could be added, but these four were the ones that helped us and, I believe, will help any school that tries them.

"But," some principals say, "I am hired to run the school, I am expected to do it, and I am held responsible." True. Nobody has said, however, how they should do it. Cooperation does not call for the negation of responsibility. The final responsibility will always be on the administrator. It is not a question of who is responsible, but of how to live with people and how a decent amount of consultation may be had. There is some risk that something untoward may happen, and the administrator must risk something on the general quality of youth. Actually the strict authoritarian runs more risks than the cooperative one, because he sets himself against others and thus sets the stage for antagonistic behavior.

"Students would just run wild and would always be asking for the impossible," says another. This is a mistaken notion of what youth are like. They tend to run wild against adults, not with them. They are most reasonable when they understand the problems of the administration. In all of the time that we operated the school council, I do not recall a single instance of student dissatisfaction when the problem was understood. It is true that the adults have to take some risks on the rightness and goodness of young people, but our bet could not be better placed.

"It wouldn't work in my school. My kids are too tough." This to me is like saying that the sicker a person is, the more important it is that he be denied curative treatment. I have gone into some detail because I believe that if cooperation worked in the Milwaukee Vocational School in 1931-1938, it will work anywhere.

The story of the School Council would not be complete without mention of the Alumni Council. This was an organization of young people who had served on the top council, and who had finished school. Each person who had been a member of the top council was invited to join the Alumni Council. Not everyone accepted, but a good many did. We soon had members of the Alumni Council living all over the city. We held our regular evening meetings at which we discussed the problems of the school and the community.

Many of the youth in school who seemed to need help were referred to whatever Alumni Council member lived in his neighborhood. The Alumni Council member called on him and attempted to serve in the capacity of big brother or sister. Of course, we had more damaged ones in some neighborhoods than in others, but in those communities we also had more Alumni Council members. Our weekly evening meetings were largely taken up with discussion of the adventures and difficulties some of our members had had and the assignment of new cases with such background as we were able to provide.

The Alumni Council was held together in part by the social aspects of membership. We had parties and dances—whatever young adults like to do. Sometimes we had weddings joining members, at which there was great celebration. This group continuously served the school as good-will representatives so that much of the bad publicity that the school suffered was allayed. The school was always subject to a certain amount of bad publicity, because many of the anti-social acts which attracted the attention of the newspapers were done by our students. After all the high schools had already sent us most of those who were likely to get into trouble. Then there were always those, as there are today, who did not believe in education for all and who were quick to blame the school.

I really watched the newspapers those days. Whenever youth was involved in crime, I would get a summons from Dr. Cooley. Were they ours? What did we know about them? Whose classes were they in? Was there anything we might have done that would have made a difference? We had many sources of information, one of the best being the Alumni Council. Quite often some member of it at least knew the family.

I shall never cease to be grateful for the loyalty and industry of those young people. Some of them must be grandparents by now. There are some I still hear from and I should like to pay tribute to them by name, but I realize the risk of missing some of the most dedicated ones. Some of them will read these words and remember.

I must not leave the subject of student participation in school government without paying tribute to the greatness of Richard Welling. Here was a giant in the earth who devoted his life and his substance to the improvement of government, particularly in the schools. He was a graduate of Harvard, a contemporary and intimate of many of the great men of that time. He became a Wall Street lawyer, but his first interest was in improving government. While a young man he and Theodore Roosevelt, a Harvard classmate, started reform movements in New York City. He fought corruption in government all his life. He was a leader in the famous Seabury investigations in New York.

Perhaps his greatest achievement, the one that cost him the most money at least, was the foundation and support of the National Self Government Committee. This committee had many famous sponsors, including John Dewey, William McAndrew, Alfred E. Smith, Lyman Beecher Stowe, and many more. There was hardly a high school principal in America who did not receive regular mail concerning democracy in school government. He was ably assisted by his secretary, Miss Sophia Pollack, who later became Mrs. Arthur Rush and now lives in Brooklyn. When Mr. Welling died about ten years ago, past ninety, little of his fortune remained, since he had spent most of it on the National Self Government Committee.

During World War I, Mr. Welling was commander of Naval Base No. 4 at Montauk, Long Island. In improving the discipline and morale of the men he put into practice the policies of democratic cooperation which he had always advocated. The results were phenomenal, although his procedures were not always approved by the Annapolis graduates.

There is a fascinating account of this, as well as of the other events in his exciting life, in his autobiography *As the Twig Is Bent.** I try not to burden this book with material found elsewhere, so I only mention this in the hope that some will get *As the Twig Is Bent* out of the library and read it.

I have dwelt long on the subject of student participation in school government. I have done this partly because I wanted to make a record of a rare adventure which has never been recorded before. I wanted to pay tribute to the young people who, often living in desperate circumstances, made it possible and gave me faith in other people, especially youth, which has supported me to this day.

Of course, student participation in school government is not the only way citizens are made. The day to day relationship between teacher and student can be a powerful factor. But in a large school such as nearly all of our urban schools have become, and with our idea that everyone must get up and hurry somewhere else every fifty minutes, it is almost impossible for everyone to feel that he is a part of the school unless some systematic way of doing it is invented. In most of our large schools today there are too many lost souls, too many of the lonely, of the unassimilated. It is perhaps a paradox that the larger the school—the more people that inhabit one city block—the more lonely a young person can be. There are a few "big wheels" who are involved in everything, but the great mass takes part in nothing. Some of these lonely souls retire into their own shells, depriving themselves of their greatest need—other human beings. Others seek friendships outside, and some form gangs which do acts that are hostile to the society which has caused their association.

I should not like to see small schools where everybody is well known to everybody else encumber themselves with a great deal of formal machinery which would only get in the way of the genuine human relationships that already exist. In a large school I do not know of any way other than a system of student participation in government by which we can make sure that everyone is included.

Youth Needs the Community

It is not only in the school that youth needs to feel involved. He yearns also to be wanted and needed by the community. When we look at our urban communities, we can see thousands of ways by which youth, now largely idle, could improve them. Many of the thoughtless

* Richard Welling, *As the Twig Is Bent* (New York: G. P. Putnam and Sons, 1942).

acts of idle youth actually cause the community to deteriorate. This is a great waste—of our money, our property, and, more particularly, our youth.

When I started writing this book, I had intended to devote a whole section of it to ways in which youth can and have participated in the improvement of their communities. But this is already going to be longer than I had intended. These ways have been written up many times in excellent form. For those who are really interested, I suggest *Learning the Ways of Democracy* published by the Educational Policies Commission of the National Education Association in 1940.* The Commission surveyed the whole country looking for ways in which youth had helped their neighborhoods. It is, as its subtitle states, a case book in civic education.

Another rich source is *Youth Serves the Community* by Paul Hanna; this book is filled with examples which can give helpful suggestions to those who want them.†

These two references will give anyone interested more suggestions than he can use. It is true that they are old, but so are the problems of youth. These problems have worsened in the twenty years since these books were written. We still have youth, more of them than ever, and we still have communities to keep up and improve.

Education for citizenship is still the primary responsibility of the home, the community, and the school. This has nothing whatever to do with whispering, or with mathematics, science, grammar, or even civics. It has to do with the way in which the young person sees himself in his relationships to those around him and to the society of which he is supposed to be a part. If he sees himself as important to the whole, as valued, many competencies will come to him, and as he gets a chance to live as though he is valued, the more valuable he will become to himself and to others.

* Educational Policies Commission, *Learning the Ways of Democracy:* A Case Book of Civic Education (Washington, D.C.: National Education Association, 1940).

† Paul Hanna, *Youth Serves the Community* (New York: Appleton-Century-Crofts, Inc., 1936).

Part III

The school is a good place for youth

Chapter 11

The Task of the School

The last part of this book will be devoted to the school. It is true that the school has been mentioned often in the first parts, because of the difficulty of discussing youth without it. Even here it will not be possible to go into detailed descriptions of programs. I have hoped from the beginning to keep this book short, so that more people (especially those educated in the good old days and who do not read very much) would read it than would be the case if it were ponderous. Actually everybody is enormously busy these days; if a book is to be read, it must be read on the run. Rather than dealing with details of programs, therefore, I shall limit myself to the ideas which make the school the way it is and to ideas which would make it a better place for youth.

As the schools are today, they are not very good places for children and youth. This is perhaps more true in the secondary than in the elementary schools; but even elementary schools have a long way to go before it can be said that they are really good places for children. There are many fine warm-hearted humanly oriented teachers in all schools, but if one were to go into the nearest classroom, either elementary or secondary, he would probably find in operation outmoded methods and procedures designed to train rather than educate. These are usually not good places for children and youth.

Since we are mostly concerned here with the problems of youth in urban living, the secondary school is of especial concern to us. Of course what is done to children in the elementary school has a great deal to do with the problems of the secondary school. And youth are more mobile than children; they are more difficult to control; they soon reach an age where they no longer can be treated as captive audiences. The secondary school simply must be a good place for all youth, because there is no other place in our society for them, and the cost in money and human resources when youth have no acceptable place is too great.

The evidences that the secondary school is not an acceptable place for all youth are many. The number who leave the school before completion is proof enough. What makes them leave when they really have no other place to go? Consider also that we do not have any real knowledge of the number of drop-outs, because all we know how to do is to count the bodies. Because of many pressures—parental, social—many stay in school physically who would be elsewhere if they could. So thousands of "drop-outs" are still in school. They have not found programs which hold meaning for them but have found it easier to "stick around" than to resist the pressures which require them to "get an education." It is a sick institution that loses forty per cent of its customers when they have no place else to go.

All over the world wherever industrialization has taken over people are paying the penalty for the displacement and rejection of youth. Delinquency is not an American phenomenon but a world-wide one. We are paying an awesome price just in police, courts, and institutions, but the greatest cost, which we do not know how to calculate, is the loss in human resources. People are being killed by youth in retaliation; parents' lives are being devastated; potential producers are becoming useless, life-long wards of the state.

If the school is to be a good place for all youth, it will need to rid itself of all forms of rejection and replace rejection with strong positive acceptance. This means acceptance of all kinds of young people so that anybody who comes to the school can feel that he not only is permitted to come, but is wanted; that here is a real place for him, and that there is something here that he can do and somebody here who cares what becomes of him. This is simple human doctrine, and it is surprising that we have not long since adopted it. It goes well with all of our various religions. Yet our detention homes and our reform schools are filled with youth who explain their plight on the ground that nobody wanted them anywhere.

We adults have worked out a complicated and effective system of rejection of youth which runs throughout our social structure. Rejection is particularly well established in our secondary schools. We have our preordained course of study, which can only be mastered by part of our intake. We have the grading system, which is designed to separate the sheep from the goats. We have our so-called social clubs, more accurately described as sororities and fraternities, in which we teach our young the more cruel aspects of rejection.* We have a powerful array of social opprobrium—teachers, peers, home, church—to pour on the person who does not fit into our adult pattern. We call them "non-conformists" or "trouble-makers." By these devices we have created a large group of second-class citizens. Some of these do not see themselves as second-class, and rebel. Some accept the judgment of others and merely sink into mediocrity.

We have even invented a new form of rejection directed toward those we prize most highly, the so-called gifted. As I pointed out earlier, one of the worst things that can happen to a young person is for his parents and teachers to judge him gifted. From then on he will be unable to lead a normal youthful life at all. His hours of labor will be greatly increased, he will be unduly penalized for small mistakes or lapses; and were it not for the fact that he is committed to higher education, he would surely give up the whole thing. So it comes about that we now have everybody rejected except a layer between the gifted and the unwanted.

The secondary school we need, then, is one where acceptance and love replace rejection; where there is enough consultation with youth so that they feel some ownership and involvement; where somebody cares about every single one of them; where there will be no second class citizens.

There are those who will claim that this is not the function of the school; that though this may be a need for youth, it must be supplied in some other place; that youth go to school to learn that which their elders decide they should know. I question the validity of this argument, but even if it is granted, where, then, shall youth be nurtured? Are these people willing to build and support a new institution for a few millions of people? Or do they prefer to just go on with a large displaced group and pay for police, courts and jails instead? If this is really what they prefer, they should understand that they cannot pay in cash for the human loss involved, but they will surely pay in the decline of a society which cannot nurture its young.

* See "Those Social Clubs," an editorial in the Tulsa *Tribune*, May 2, 1959, by Jenkin Lloyd Jones.

Chapter 12

The Attackers

It is necessary here to devote some space to those who are attacking the schools through speeches, books, magazine articles, newspapers, television, radio—all of the avenues by which the public may be reached. This is not a particularly pleasant task, but it must be done because the attackers are harming youth. Anything which harms youth is germane to this document.

I think that if adults want to carry on a vendetta, they should do it in such a way that the old, the sick, the infirm or the young will not be involved. The attacks on education have been among adults all right, but they have caused teachers to become more rejecting of youth rather than more accepting. It seems we might find some other dry bone to fight over, if we must unload our hostility.

The attackers are legion when one considers all the magazines and newspaper editorials. I have not devoted my life to a study of what they have to say, but since they are so ever-present no one can avoid them. A list of the attackers could be pages long, but if it were, it would not contain the name of a single person who has made a study of teaching and learning. I suspect that this is the only area in the whole of human knowledge where it seems to be granted that those who have not studied the problem, who are unfamiliar with the available research data, are generally accepted as knowing more about it than those who have.

I do not know whether or not the current crop of attackers see themselves as first in the fray to save our country. Since they are obviously unfamiliar with the literature in this field, they may not know that scapegoating youth is as old as human history. They may see themselves as original saviors. Methods of teaching, though they change more slowly than anything I can think of in our culture, have always been under attack by those who do not teach.

I think it will not serve us to go back into antiquity for evidence of this. The following is taken from the News Letter, March, 1959, published by the Bureau of Educational Research at the Ohio State University, Columbus, Ohio, and edited by Edgar Dale and Hazel Gibbony.

> When we were mere boys, boys had to do a little work in school. They were not coaxed; they were hammered. Spelling, writing and arithmetic were not electives; and you had to learn. In these more fortunate times, elementary education has become in many places a sort of vaudeville show. The child must be kept amused and learns what he pleases. Many sage teachers scorn the old-fashioned rudiments; and it seems to be regarded as between a misfortune and a crime for a child to learn to read and spell by the old methods. Vast and fruitful intellects have devoted themselves to child study and child psychology. "Visualized" reading and other great inventions have come in. . . . We "spring" an examination on little Johnnie when he comes home from school and find that he can't spell "cat" without a picture of pussy before him or that he spells it "mew."

This could easily have fallen from the pen of one of our current crop of attackers. It is taken, however, from the New York *Sun* dated October 5, 1902. I was then in the second grade, and hence must be one of the blighted. It was before John Dewey had had a chance to cast his evil spell. Here is education in "the good old days," to which so many look with nostalgia.

If our current attackers see themselves as original leaders of a great movement, they might be shocked to know who their immediate predecessors were. In the years immediately following World War II, while the Communist hysteria was at its height, the attackers were mainly fascist. They were led by Allen Zoll, who put a spurious Ph.D. after his name, and who was a prime factor in the sad affair at Pasadena, California. His method of operation was to set group against group, religion against religion, race against race. He apparently made a living by organizing associations, collecting dues, and selling pamphlets. He was the organizer of American Patriots Inc., which appeared on the Attorney General's list as fascist. He had many fascist associates, and for a long time they did a great deal of harm to youth. Those who want to know more about them should read "Who's Trying to Ruin Our Schools" by Arthur D. Morse in the September 1951 issue of *McCall's*.

These attackers receded, as have the others before them. Though we are perhaps in more peril from communism than ever, the public has grown tired of the subject, especially as espoused by fascists. Though the fascists have dropped the cudgel, it has not been permitted to lie idle. It has been grasped and teachers and youth are being flailed by a new crop. Let me state here that I am not implying that the new crop is fascist, as was their predecessor. They seem rather to be people who observe that our youth are getting some pleasure out of life and are disturbed by this fact. Some of them have had the living daylights scared out of them by the Russian sputnik and are plainly scapegoating to keep from facing the fact of adult failure.

These are indeed frightening days, and I would be the last to deny it. I do not like to realize that the two most powerful nations in the world have learned how to destroy each other and that life on this earth could be terminated by someone outside our control. But to cry out against those who were barely born when decisions affecting these matters were made, to become angry because our schools are not prisons, seems an odd reaction. Perhaps it would not be too far-fetched to conjecture that this crop of attackers has taken its counsel from fear, and, as always happens under such circumstances, has struck out blindly. Their handling of data would support this supposition. Zoll and his associates did not take their counsel from fear. They apparently wanted a fascist state, were willing to use any means to get it, and knew that first they would have to destroy our system of education for all. That is why they accused teachers of teaching subversion without even knowing they were doing it (see *McCall's*).

In the spring of 1958 a small group of professors from two universities met to consider the effects of the attack on education and on youth.* This was about six months after the Russians had launched their first satellite, as a result of which Americans were humiliated. It was shortly after *Life*'s reckless blast against education. Admiral Rickover was using taxpayers' money, through the Atomic Energy Commission, to broadcast his opinions through the mails. Of course the Admiral has the right to say anything he wants to; he even has the right to abuse the scientific method; but I wonder if he had the right to make me, as a taxpayer, pay the postage.

It was shortly after a nationally televised program had left the impression that every boy in a certain school was taking "co-ed cooking."

The group of professors drew up the statement which follows. Since this is a quotation from their document, there may be some repetition of ideas already expressed.

I. *The attackers have abandoned democracy.*

(a) They have repudiated the dream of America which holds that each individual is worthy, has value to the rest of us, and has a right to opportunity to achieve the maximum within his capacity. They have

* Professors Fred G. Walcott of the University of Michigan and T. D. Rice, M. J. Clute, J. W. Menge, and the author, from Wayne State University.

advocated the creation of a worthy and a worthless class establishing an intellectual elite bringing into being a class of the educationally disinherited. Thus they have repudiated and denounced democratic principles and espoused feudalistic and royalistic principles.

They may deny this by saying that they are in favor of schools or classes for the stupid, but no American will long attend a school where he is a second-class citizen.

(b) They have demanded a return to the educational methods of the old world, in the face of the fact that most Americans or their ancestors fled the old world to escape offensive and inhuman ideologies best represented by their schools; in face of the fact that many Europeans wish they could emulate the American public school system. Some have openly advocated that we imitate Russian schools. Only a short time ago the same people would have cried out against such advocates as being subversive and un-American.

(c) By casting doubt in the public mind as to the values of universal education, they have made it difficult to finance public education. Securing sufficient funds to carry out the American dream of universal education has always been difficult, and these attacks have made it much more so.

II. *They have asked us to emphasize preparation for war more than for peace.*

(a) Some of them have demanded that every child who is to receive a good education be highly trained in science and mathematics as the only means to our salvation. This excessive emphasis has to be at the expense of learning the ways of peace. The humanities—the arts, music, literature, the appreciation of the life good to live, preparation for the constructive use of leisure—have no place in their plans.

III. *They have taken their counsel from fear.*

(a) Since Russia launched the first satellite they have become frightened and have exhibited behavior in keeping with this destructive emotion; instead of criticizing the Congress, the military, or the Commander-in-Chief, who might have been able to "beat Russia", they have turned their wrath on the weakest and most defenseless group in our society, our youth and their teachers. They have increased the hostility of adults toward youth.

(b) They have demanded that youth be used as means to adult ends. Although they are frightened, they do not call on adults to work longer hours. It is the old story of old people making wars that youth has to fight. They do not consult youth, do not include them in the body-politic. The concept that youth belongs to the state is typical nazi and communist doctrine, and it is inimical to democracy. They have further attacked all youth by taking examples of delinquency and using these examples to incriminate all.

IV. *They have violated the standards of moral integrity.*

(a) They have violated the canons of rational inquiry. The scientist, the scholar, should above all be rational and speak from data. When intellectuals fail to be rational, when they make judgments with false or inadequate data, they destroy confidence in the intellectual. It is anti-intellectualism in its most insidious form.

(b) They have stooped to deliberate dishonesty. For example, they have cut film, including only the part they wanted, and broadcast it. They have thrust a frivolous magazine into the hands of a high school girl and then photographed her and broadcast the picture all over the world, representing it as typical. This is reminiscent of campaign methods used by McCarthy in Maryland.

(c) They have stooped to the device of name-calling and the use of color-words loaded with emotion.

(d) They have attacked the integrity of whole groups, not by individuals but in mass. They have implied that teachers, superintendents, principals, and teacher trainers do not want good schools, but are really plotting America's downfall. They have condemned all those who are responsible for the present program as either knaves or fools.

(e) They have ignored the scientific data which show that our youth of comparable capacity to learn know more, read and cipher better, do better on tests than they ever have.

(f) They have ignored all that is known of human nature and human psychology. For example, they have denied the fact of uniqueness. They have called for standardization. They have demanded conformity in the name of rugged individualism. They have shown ignorance or deliberate disregard of research in child growth and development, retention, and transfer of training.

(g) They have failed to assume responsibility for their own acts. What is the moral effect of forcing large numbers of youth out of school? How would this affect our delinquency problems, our police departments, the safety of our homes? What would become of the educationally disinherited? What are the moral consequences of forcing an adolescent to take a course in higher mathematics without regard to his capacity to learn? The attackers never move on to consequences.

V. *They have rendered our teachers less able.*

(a) They have made hundreds of thousands of good teachers, who stand heroically in the classroom year after year doing their best, to doubt themselves, causing them to be less able to meet great difficulties. They have caused good teachers to be more punitive. They have brought out the worst in punitive teachers.

(b) They have ridiculed and condemned the constructive efforts of teachers to correct the recognized abuses of the educational system and to carry out required changes. People who work conscientiously in any walk of life become aware of malfunctions brought about by changing conditions and demanding adaptations in the light of new research. In response to these insistent demands they institute experimental procedures designed to correct and improve what can be no longer tolerated. The enemies of education have misrepresented these constructive efforts as deliberate conspiracies to debase the quality of the schools.

(c) They have distorted and misrepresented the extent of adaptive and remedial measures which are designed to correct the maladjustments of slow-learning or mentally-retarded children. Special features maintained for a small minority of the pupils such as "opportunity rooms," remedial reading classes, and classes in cosmetology or rug-weaving have been alleged to represent the whole curriculum of the school and to dilute the offerings available to capable and academically-minded pupils.

(d) They have discouraged teachers from taking continuing courses in education and advanced degrees in professional subjects such as guidance and counseling, child development, special education, and secondary school teaching. They allege an established racket maintained by schools of education playing hand-in-glove with state licensing agencies. They have decried the very existence of professional training, claiming that nothing beyond a knowledge of a subject is necessary for teaching—as though the profession through the centuries has developed no special knowledge of psychology, the laws of learning, human growth and development, techniques of teaching, and ways of coping with environmental conditions essential to teaching (Example: The myth of method without subject matter).

I have devoted some space to the attackers, not because they have attacked adults, but because they have hurt youth. Those of us engaged in education have many faults, although we are not accused of the ones which data will support. But this book is about youth, and anything which damages youth is properly included here.

Recalling the main thesis of Part III, the school, and particularly the secondary school, must be a good place for all youth. This is held to be true because urban youth, which includes most of them, have no other place in our society.

The attackers have made the school less suitable for youth because they have frightened teachers. Teachers are being more and more "tough" on youth, demanding more homework, allowing less and less leisure for youth, and, in the name of high standards, giving less reward. In fact, the high school students who do what their teachers tell them to have virtually no leisure at all. They do not even get the amount of sleep which is required for good health. This is particularly true if a student has been proscribed as gifted. Some teachers have "raised their standards" merely by lowering grades. It comes about that youth are being required to do many more hours of work and are receiving lower grades. What these teachers have really lowered is the quality of the school as a human institution, and they have reduced their ability to provide a place in which youth will not need to feel unwanted.

The attackers have made teachers more cautious and more fearful of any issue that might be controversial. This is a serious threat to the right to know. Freedom to learn is surely one of the basic freedoms in a democracy. So our teachers deal almost exclusively with issues which are dead and do not matter.

A newspaper item recently stated that in 1959 all categories of building are ahead of 1958 except school building. The attackers have succeeded in creating the impression that school people have been wasting their money, with the result that communities have refused to provide funds even to build the needed classrooms to shelter their own young, not to mention the need for more and better paid teachers. This is happening in spite of the fact that there is a tidal wave of youth approaching high school age, accountable to the increased birth rate in the post-war years. The attackers are not responsible for all of the financial hardship which schools are enduring at a time when we are more prosperous than ever. It seems probable that they are partly responsible, but it is only fair to note that the American people have always been penurious in their support of education. The attackers surely are entitled to some credit for the large size of classes, the half-day sessions, and particularly the elimination of many features of the curriculum such as art and music. The parts of the school program which have contributed most to the life good to live for youth have usually been the first to go, under the austerity economy forced on boards of education. We see the spectacle of our most important democratic institution starving to death in the midst of plenty.

Chapter 13

Our False Assumptions

Unless we are coerced by someone who has power over us, what we do reveals our real beliefs. If we fail to provide for our young under urban conditions, it means that we do not really think they need care, or we are not concerned about them. If we have over-crowded and often hostile schools, it is because we think this is good enough, or that hostility toward youth is good for them.

In my opinion, the general public harbors many false beliefs. These stand in the way of providing the proper nurture of our young. Until we surrender these false beliefs and acquire some more accurate and humane ones, it will be difficult indeed to provide decent growing conditions for those we procreate.

I am not now writing about the attackers, although they attack because they hold many of these notions, and they flourish because so many of the people concur in them. I do not consider most attackers to be insincere. They are usually uninformed and hold outmoded ideas about the nature of the young human organism and how it learns, what it responds to, what it fights.

Below is a list of assumptions which seem to be more or less generally held, not only by "the man on the street," but unfortunately by many teachers. Not all of these assumptions are held by everybody, of course, but it is my opinion that each one is widely enough held so that it does damage to the cause of youth.

1) *Many people believe that children and youth are constitutionally opposed to learning.* This includes also the belief that children and youth are worse than when we were young. This has been considered in Part I. It logically follows that we must get tough with our young. If they are just being contrary, then we must coerce them. It is generally assumed that there is nothing wrong with youth that a good beating will not cure.

The daily press is filled with evidence of this attitude. Recently, a juvenile court judge announced that his cure for delinquency is a couple of weeks in solitary confinement. A prison warden says that the severest punishment they ever used with desperate adult criminals was three days' of solitary confinement. The press reported later that the judge got thousands of letters praising his idea. Adult hatred of youth breaks out in volume whenever it has a chance.

The notion that the young do not want to learn is disputed by the very nature of learning. Learning is an integral part of growth; it is a product of experience and is as continuous as experience. Learning leads to more learning as the purposive human organism makes its way. What infuriates adults is that the young do not always want to learn what we want them to. Resistance to these adult purposes is often caused by the behavior of adults.

As for the efficacy of punishment as a cure, one cannot help wondering how long the otherwise good people of the world will cling to the notion that it ever settles anything. It is true that we do not use violence as a cure as much as we used to. Men have been hanged for stealing a loaf of bread, but there is ample evidence that capital punishment does not reduce crime. In the early days of our own country, the whipping post was standing in many villages. It is not uncommon today to see in the press demands for its return, usually for youth only.

I think there is no real evidence that anyone ever was improved by a flogging, and plenty of evidence that the vast majority of our delinquents have been brutalized from infancy. Of course, it is true that when a gang of delinquents, for example, go on an anti-social rampage, the police have to stop them. But when they are stopped, a good beating or a couple of weeks in solitary confinement will not prevent their future anti-social behavior. If we provided the proper nurture for our young, such gang activities would not occur.

2) *Many people believe that anybody can learn anything if he tries.* This is the basis for our culture valuing so highly the standard academic curriculum. It is the cause of great strife between parents and their young. For many parents hold unrealistic ambitions for their young. Most often the parents want their children to become medical doctors. This is not hard to understand when one considers the financial returns. It may be a drive for old age insurance on the part of the parents.

If parents believe this, it again calls for coercion and conflict, with all of their attendant evils. It causes teachers endless trouble, when junior cannot acquire entrance to a medical school, or whatever else parents hold dear. It is a denial of the scientific fact of uniqueness, which nature has gone to so much trouble to insure.* It is a good thing that human beings *are* unique, else we could not do anything at all.

There are some in our society who would say that they do not believe that anybody can learn anything, but that those who cannot do not matter. The school should ignore them, freeze them out, or not even admit them. Where these are to go they do not say.

3) *Many believe that democracy will not work in the schools.* Democracy is soft, and what we need is to make our young tough, by giving them tough treatment. We should copy the schools of totalitarian states.

Unfortunately, many teachers hold this belief. It is not uncommon to hear a teacher say, "I've tried democracy, and it won't work." Thus dismissing the basic tenet of our culture, they resort to old methods which help them to achieve certain short-time goals, such as a quiet room with everyone looking down at a book. This teacher then often gets praise from his superiors and the parents of his children, confirming him in his autocratic beliefs and actions. It is hard for this teacher to realize that by this method he has shut off most of the possibility for significant learning to take place. Anyway, the teacher is more comfortable when he has all of his learners "under control," and since schools are most often adult-centered, the comfort of the one adult in the room assumes considerable importance.

Of course, if a young person reaches the age of fifteen without ever having experienced a democratic atmosphere, he has no way to understand it, and the teacher who says to such a group of youth, "Now let's all be democratic" will have trouble. Democracy is a way of life calling for mutual respect and consultation, among other things. It has to be learned, as all else has to be learned. If a group of fifteen-year-olds have never known mutual respect, they have to begin in small ways to learn a new way of living and working together.

This is not easy. It is best accomplished when the democratic way of life pervades the home into which the infant is born. If it is then continued through kindergarten and the elementary grades, when he reaches the secondary school the youth will be at home in a democratic atmosphere, will know how to behave, indeed will find it difficult and offensive to be expected to behave otherwise.

The democratic way of life is not easy. It demands self-discipline, which is much more difficult to practice than discipline from without. The easiest way is simply to be told what to do and to follow orders.

* Earl C. Kelley, "The Significance of Being Unique," *ETC., The Journal of General Semantics* (Spring, 1957).

This hardly prepares one for democratic citizenship. Democracy is not soft, but strengthening to one's moral fibre. The earlier a child can come into this way of life, the more competent he will be. Anarchy may be soft, but it should not be confused with democracy.

It is an odd feature of our culture that most adults cherish freedom for themselves but think it is bad for their young. As adults, they are usually ready to "come out swinging" if a neighbor impinges on their rights of freedom. These same people seem to think that while tyranny is bad for them, it is good for their young.

Not too many people, I think, really believe that we should copy the European schools. These are the schools that trained the people who have plunged the world into war again and again. These are the schools which have produced a nation which now not only threatens peace, but the destruction of all life on the earth. These are the schools which so stifled liberty that our ancestors fled from them, preferring the unknown terrors of the American wilderness.

Some current attackers strongly advocate the return of the European form of education, with its aristocracy and its peon class. I doubt that they will get many followers on this particular point, but it is a good idea to say here that the schools of any society will in the long run have to be in accordance with the tenets of that society. We cannot have authoritarian schools as exemplified by totalitarian states without losing our democratic form of government and our individual adult freedoms. The skeletal form of democratic government may persist for a while, but even that will succumb eventually if it is not fed by youth's understanding as youth becomes adult. This is why one whole part of this book is devoted to education for democratic citizenship.

4) *Many believe that no learning can take place without pain.* This leads to the belief that if pain is not present in a learning situation, it is our duty to induce it. It follows that anything is good that is hard to do.

It is this belief which causes so many people to resent it whenever they see young people enjoying themselves at school or when they "ought" to be doing their homework. School and homework just about account for all of youth's time. It is this belief which makes so many people attack what they call frills. A frill apparently is anything which the adult did not have an opportunity to experience when he was young.

All of this raises the interesting question as to what is hard. If a person wants and needs to do anything of considerable size, such as a piece of research where sources have to be looked up, parts of it will be hard to do. For example, in writing this book in defense of youth, if I wanted to make the point that the attackers are harming youth, I had to read a considerable part of their writing. No one could read all of them, but much time had to be spent in this manner. This I found to be onerous labor. But this hardness was an inherent and necessary part of my original undertaking. It was not thought up by somebody else and inflicted on me because it was good for me. The very nature of life is hard, but it makes a great deal of difference whether it is inherent in what we are doing or forced upon us for the good of our souls.

Since we believe that hardness is a good in itself, many courses which exist in our high schools are inflicted on our youth for the very reason that we believe that it is good for youth to suffer. Not that these courses are bad or evil in themselves. No course is bad in itself. It depends on how and why and on whom it is used. What can be a delight to one person may be torture to another. The notion that the so-called academic courses are hard and the others are easy will not stand examination.

Some current attackers are among many who hold to this notion. They therefore serve as good illustrations of this point. Perhaps they would have no trouble earning top grades in so-called academic courses. But could they do it if the specialties were switched? Perhaps, but not surely. Many historians are poor physicists, and so on. To exaggerate this point, since nothing infuriates the attackers as much as the sight of a drum majorette, why not transfer them to this role, and have them learn to perform these functions, including throwing a baton twenty feet into the air and catching it with a finger so that the baton can continue to twirl, all without losing step with the band. A whole new concept of what is hard might emerge.

It comes about that that activity which one knows how to do, enjoys doing, and sees purpose in doing is easy. That which one has no taste for, or competence in, and sees no value in, becomes hard.

This brings up the whole question of frills. This word, and the word "new-fangled" have come to be used in a manner intended to make the reader think frills are bad, wasteful, useless, unnecessary. A frill is something added, usually to a drapery or a dress, to make it look better though not essential to its function. It is not properly used with regard to any part of the curriculum. It may be applied to school buildings or fixtures where an effort has been made to improve their appearance and make them more attractive and inviting. It might not even be proper here, for if the school is to serve what I hold to be its function, the building must be inviting to both young and adult. When anything becomes essential to the function for which it is designed, then it cannot be called a frill.

As for frills in the curriculum, what may be unnecessary for one learner may be quite essential to another. A course in higher mathematics is quite essential to some people, but utterly useless to others. The frills then come to depend upon the point of view of each individual. Surely we can see that if the school is to be an institution inviting to all youth, it must be not merely good to look at and comfortable, from both physical and human considerations, but it will have to have broad opportunities in the way of activities. Thus there will always be programs which suit some youth and are superfluous to others.

In spite of the taxpayers' refusal in many communities to approve bond issues for new schools, caused in part I believe by the attackers, a good many new schools have been built since about 1950. Many of these schools are beautiful. This seems to hurt some of our citizens. Nearly all of the schools built before 1930 (virtually none were built in the 30's or 40's) had no beauty built into them. Then they were painted inside a sort of schoolhouse drab—a mixture of green and gray. Some say that the decorators, to save money, took all of the paint they had left, poured it together, and put it on the hallways. This seems improbable, since by that method there would be some variation from school to school. Whatever the cause, schools of that period, through a combination of architectural monstrosity and school-drab paint, were made about as repulsive as they could be.

Beauty in architecture and decorating has come into American lives for almost the first time. It is now expected and almost required in all public buildings, as well as in office buildings and factories. Hard-headed businessmen have at last learned that it does not pay profits to build factories which are purely utilitarian. The old industrial plant, with its sordid appearance, its dirt, mud, and grime, is a thing of the past. It is gone because these conditions reduce production, lower morale and cause employees to be irritable and discontented. How long will we go on complaining about the cost of beauty built into our schools, and calling for the return of the school-drab building "which was plenty good enough when I was a boy"?

Hardness for hardness' sake is contradictory to the education and development of the free human organism. It cannot be applied anyway except to a captive group. This the secondary school does not have. The factory owner has more of a captive group, through economic necessity, than does the school. If hardness is a good, and I hold that it is neither good nor bad but inherent in most things people want to do, then we must find a better way to bring it about than simply imposing it for its own sake.

5) *Too many people have unbounded faith in the old curriculum,* which consists mainly of English, history, science, foreign language, and mathematics. They believe that these are educative in themselves, that once we get them inside the learner, he will automatically be educated. All else are frills.

I do not mean to imply that these so-called disciplines are bad in themselves. They are very good for many learners. But to insist upon them for those who cannot profit from them is another act of exclusion or rejection, and these subjects become the rocks upon which many are broken. The possibilities of human growth have increased enormously in modern times. There are many other ways now through which one may have facilitating experiences. They neglect or do not provide for the development of moral social sense. They may indeed be administered in such a way as to place a premium on dishonesty.

The German people under Hitler were perhaps the most literate, the best educated in these disciplines, of any people in the world. Yet this "education" did not prevent the rise of one of the most dangerous and pernicious governments ever known. They not only killed millions of those whom they saw as enemies, but millions of their own people. It was possible in this "educated" populace, to fan the flames of darkest prejudice against a large group of their own nationals, condemning millions to mass torture and execution. Any education which allows such prejudice to survive cannot be called by that name. The fact is that these disciplines have little or nothing to do with what seems to me to be central in human development. These are the ability to contrive one's way out of unique dilemmas, the courage to do so, consciousness of the need for others, integrity in one's relationship with self and others, all related to the life good to live, and only incidentally related to the "disciplines."

This seems a good time to make a statement about foreign language. There is a good deal of uncritical thinking abroad in the land on this matter. We are often malodorously compared to other countries on this subject. It is often said that in European schools everyone is forced to learn English, at least, in addition to his native tongue. Of course this is not true, since almost no European country tries to educate everybody. What we lose sight of is that these countries are relatively small compared to ours, and other languages impinge upon the people far more than is true here. It is also true that English is more a universal language than any other. There is far more probability that a Hollander, for example, will have an opportunity to use English than that an American will need Dutch.

It would be a fine thing if our world were so constructed that every American could have a chance to talk many languages, and had need to do so. That would call for a mixture of peoples far beyond what we now have. But to force our young to master even one language without any prospect of using it is pure discipline, hardness for hardness' sake. In the first place, the way language is usually taught results in pure memory work, and rarely enables one to read and speak the language with sufficient facility to be functional in a foreign country. Then if the learner should become facile in one language, he might never leave this country, or if he does, he is quite likely to go to the wrong foreign country. Thus his learning such as it is will deteriorate through disuse, and he will be left with nothing but the memory of several years of hard work.

Any educated person, if he wants to, can learn enough of almost any language in three months so that he will be able to communicate in whatever country he plans to go to. Under these conditions, he will be motivated to learn, and his learning will have immediate use and an opportunity to grow. If we think about what goes on in a secondary school in this area, we can only justify it on the ground that it is good because it is hard. This we have to reject as a respectable reason, since just making things hard for youth is a form of rejection.

6) *Most people believe that it is possible to determine early who is "able,"* and that it is good to separate them out from the rest. They have great faith in the I.Q. test as an instrument for such selection. They think that democratic leaders attain their power in the absence of those to be led. They also believe that the brighter a person is, the longer he needs to work, and that hours spent and learning achieved equate.

"Education for the gifted" is a social symptom which has swept over our country in recent years. It is really a symptom of fear and lack of faith in democracy. It seeks to establish a class that will lead and one that will follow. It is a negation of the concept that every American shall have equal opportunity to reach his potential.

It is true that many people are unaware of the full implications of separating out those whom adults deem to be "superior." These are outcomes which logically follow. The implications of these separations for democracy are serious, since democracy can only survive when it is based on the involvement and participation of everybody.

Adults do not seem to be conscious of the reaction when somebody says to one child "You are gifted" and to another "You are not gifted." The glibness with which school people do this never ceases to astound me. One would think that the adults who do this would suffer agony, particularly because there must be many borderline cases even with their so-called objective criteria. Further, I am amazed that more school buildings are not burned by parents when they discover that their cherished ones have been judged to be unworthy of the best their country has to provide. It would be just as logical for the parents of a child which has been judged as "gifted" to resent and resist the label. Their child will not then have the gift of a normal childhood, and will be given a concept of self which on the whole will be damaging.

There is some effort, of course, to keep this information from the gifted and the backward. I doubt that this ever succeeds. It is a sad commentary on how backward adults think all children and youth are.

Some people believe that it is possible to select the future leaders as early as the elementary grades. It is shocking to contemplate that even such little ones should be dedicated to adult purposes. These people seem to have great faith in the deluge of tests now flooding our schools, put out by commercial institutions interested in sales and profits rather than in children. This seems particularly true of the I.Q. test.

The I.Q. test was "sold" to the American people during the first part of this century. By means of this test it was supposed possible to determine within one per cent what any person's "intelligence" was, and that this was constant throughout life. This was a very handy gadget. Teachers could tell whom not to expect anything of. There were many abuses, which I believe are no longer committed. In some schools in the 20's, pupils' scores were posted on the bulletin board. Many teachers used these scores for grading, that is, a child with an I.Q. of 80 must not be given an A, because he could not possibly have earned it, and other teachers might raise their eyebrows. Children who received low scores were really condemned from then on, although the testing methods were most unscientific.

Scientific researchers began to question the validity of the I.Q. scores, especially since intelligence had never been satisfactorily defined. In 1932 we had the Iowa studies, under the direction of Professor George Stoddard. These showed in brief that an individual's I.Q. varies, depending upon the kind of life he is able to live. Rich human environments raise individual scores, while starved environments lower them. We have known, then, for thirty years that one's I.Q. is at least in part a product of the quality of the life he has led. Despite this knowledge, we see now a revival of faith in the I.Q. score. The dead hand of the past is heavy upon us.

To apply these tests to young children is particularly horrifying. Even babies are sometimes subjected to them. Unreliable at all ages, the tests become less and less reliable the younger the child is. If we want to live happily with our young, little good can come from such testing.

Those who would select our elite early fail to take into account the well-known fact that individuals mature at different ages and at different rates. Many individuals are late in maturing. Some bloom early and then seem to fade. Potentialities are impossible to detect, because they do not even appear until situations call them up. This varying rate of development is especially true in adolescence.

Proponents of isolation of the gifted say that gifted children are bored in the ordinary class and waste their time. In the degree that this is true, it is of course regrettable. I do not want anybody to be bored, and I am afraid that many of our classes not only bore the gifted but everybody else. The fault here is in the manner of teaching. We are strongly persuaded that in a given class everybody must learn the same thing. If this is true, it will not be possible for the teacher to please everybody under any circumstances. Even the so-called gifted vary too much for this to be possible. The idea that everyone in a class must or can learn the same thing is based on an out-moded concept of the nature of knowledge, of learning and of teaching. No two persons ever learn exactly the same thing anyway, or ever can.

If a class is taught so that the potentialities of each learner can be properly developed, then the so-called gifted lose as much from separation as do those judged not to be gifted. They lose the unique contributions of many others, besides losing their opportunities to develop leadership. If these gifted, selected by batteries of tests, are indeed our future leaders, then they need to stay where they can develop skills in working with others; and where they will not be deprived of others.

Many people think that in order to prepare youth for college, it is necessary to separate the college-bound from the others. I do not concede that preparation for college is a desirable objective of the secondary school, since I hold that the secondary school must be a good place for all youth. Studies have been made, however, which show that when students of similar capacities and interests are compared, the students from schools having special classes for the gifted do no better in college than comparable students from schools which do not isolate the gifted.

It is true that in a school which depends upon individual counseling, certain groupings always occur. For example, only a small percentage of any student body would be in a trigonometry class. They would be the ones who have ability in higher mathematics. But the big difference is that these learners have more or less selected themselves, to get what they want and need. The same could be said for all advanced specializations.

It makes all the difference whether this process is a natural one, or is imposed from without. I believe that in all walks in life, including education, forced segregation is an evil, a denial of the right of a human being to achieve a place for himself, implicit in a democratic society.

7) *Most people do not comprehend the deep significance of each human being's uniqueness.* This seems clear not by what people say, but what they do. It is odd, too, because the very foundation of democracy must rest on this fact.

It is too easy to say that of course anybody looking at a classroom filled with learners can see that no two are alike. The fact that they are different in *every* way, that they cannot and will not learn the same things, goes much deeper than mere appearance.

Nature went to enormous trouble to bring about uniqueness. In schools an equally enormous effort is made to bring about similarity and conformity. This is never accomplished, because of the nature of the human organism. We never cease trying, although if we count our losses, we can see that it is a losing battle. Each individual is built out of unique experience, unique purpose, and unique perception. Such knowledge as he possesses is unlike that of any other, because he has to relate it to a unique personality.

This causes a great deal of trouble for the authoritarian teacher who sees his role as one who brings about the same outcomes in all his learners. He never succeeds although he never knows how greatly different the outcomes really are.

The fact is that, though uniqueness poses a problem for the teacher who lives for the same outcomes for all learners, it is the individual's most valuable asset. The ways in which he is different from all others is his reason-to-be. The fact that each individual has something, knows something which nobody else has or knows, is the precise reason why no man is expendable; why it is that when anyone is lost, we all lose. If human beings were not unique, nobody could contribute anything to anybody, because all would have the same. There is no such thing as really surrendering one's individuality in any normal situation. It may happen in war prison camps where brainwashing techniques are used, but it does not even happen in the penitentiaries where the possibilities for outside stimulation are greatly reduced.

Because uniqueness is not truly understood and accepted, some people think it is bad for people to work together. They say that it works toward uniformity and mediocrity. They do not seem to realize that when people work together, they have the benefit of each other's unique gifts and talents. The benefits are always to the individual as he goes about the complicated business of living. When people work together they of course cannot always have their own way, but nobody can have that in a democratic society. The only way in which a person can have his own way completely is in isolation. But then he is deprived of other people, and lacks that on which he must feed.

The full acceptance of the scientific fact that each human being is unique would greatly modify present educational practice, and make our schools better places for all youth.

8) *Most people have a false concept of what is possible in the way of establishing and maintaining standards.* They think that standards are something which lie outside of the learner, and can be applied to all. It is peculiar that they do not think such outside standards can be applied to all activities, but that it is possible in academic matters. They would not, for example, expect all to reach a given standard in running a hundred yards. They can see that some cannot run at all. They do not see that this same incapacity can exist in what they call matters of the mind.

An unworkable idea of the nature of standards has caused teachers and learners more trouble, perhaps, than any other. Young people have been broken by it, and it has embittered many teachers who cannot help feeling frustration at their repeated failure to reach their standards. This makes both young and old less adequate as human beings.

The secondary schools before World War I were small, highly selective, and had in them mostly only those who were somewhat academically inclined. Teachers became accustomed to the use of standards that lay outside the learner, and the enormity of this error was not apparent. Beginning in about 1920, however, the American people began to believe in secondary education for all. This brought in youth the like of whom the teachers had never seen. They of course did not know what to do about many of their students except to exhort and coerce them to learn that which they were not willing or able to study. This coercion caused many to leave school. Too many stayed, however, for the old curriculum and the old standards to be workable.

The teachers (and I was one of them) did not know any way to meet this situation but to lower their standards. The result of this was that the courses of study became so simple that they were virtually useless. This is what the attackers call the "watered-down curriculum." It is my opinion that the schools in this instance have done this, that it is a valid criticism. It is valid by accident, however, since the critics usually did not bother to visit any schools. Perhaps this proves that if a critic makes charges enough in the absence of data, he cannot fail to be right once in a while.

The reason for the watered-down curriculum is that the teachers could see that they had to make adjustments to the changing nature of their students, and they did not know that there was any other way.

Teachers are so accustomed to the routine of the textbook, the assignment, the recitation and the evaluation that it is hard for them to think of teaching in any other way. When they were confronted by the problems presented when all youth came to school, so established was this ritual that the only part the teacher could move was the standard. This being established by adults outside of the learners was movable. Standards were therefore lowered.

Another strange phenomenon is that some teachers think they can raise standards simply by lowering grades and increasing homework. We have the sad spectacle of high school youth working many hours into the night, having scarcely any leisure, and being downgraded for their pains. The brighter the student, the more he has to work, the more repetition he is subjected to. Enrichment becomes more of the same.

There is another way by which variation in human competence can be dealt with. Instead of lowering standards the teacher might have abandoned the idea that in a given class everyone has to study the same thing and come out with the same results. As long as the teacher clings to the "one lesson" concept, he will always miss some of his learners. The lesson may be aimed at the top, the middle, or the bottom, but since human beings are unique, it cannot fit all. Release from the "one lesson" ideal would call for new methods of teaching, but present knowledge of human nature and learning call for this. The abandonment of the notion that subject matter is a good in itself would be liberating to all teachers and to all those who goad teachers.

Subject matter is of course essential to the learning process. Nobody can learn without learning something. No method can be used without something to use it on. All human knowledge is good if it is used properly. The question is "Who is it good for, and when, and why?" Methods and subject matter are not a duality. Nobody teaches without subject matter, and everybody has a method.

There is, however, no item of subject matter which everybody has to have in order to live adequate useful lives. If anyone doubts this, let him name one, and I will point to successful people who do not have it. Now some will say that I do not believe that people should learn to read. The excessive pressure that our young are subjected to for the sake of reading is debatable. But reading is a skill, a very valuable one, and not an item of subject matter. Confusion of skills and subject matter has compounded our education problems.

People who attempt to humanize education are often accused of having no standards. This is nonsense. Everybody has standards, just as everybody has values. It makes a difference, though, whether the standard is outside of the learner or whether it is within him. It makes a difference whether one cherishes his geometry or his youngsters. If we abandon the concept that everyone has to learn the same thing, we then can have different standards for different people. Scientific research indicates that this is not a notion but a requirement. What teachers need is human standards, not material ones. A standard to hold on to, it seems to me, is that every human being should have the opportunity to develop his own unique potentialities, so that the full meaning of being human can emerge. This can never be achieved by applying a flat outside standard to everyone, accepting those who reach it and rejecting those who do not. It makes no difference whether this outside standard is in mathematics, science, foreign language, English, art, music, or foot-racing.

9) *Most lay people and indeed many teachers believe that the mind is something separate from the body, and can be trained independently.*

This is what is known in the trade as "faculty psychology." The mind is not only separate from and independent of the body, but it is further divided, so that there is a separate seat of memory, the will, and so on. This idea is so ancient that it is difficult to abandon. Long before the first psychologists came into being, these beliefs were held. They have been completely abandoned by all psychologists, who make scientific studies of such matters. This is another belief that was born in mysticism and antiquity, but which has been entirely refuted by scientific research. Such refutation, unfortunately, does not uproot it from the beliefs of men, on which social institutions operate.

Faculty psychology is the cause, I believe, of the training concept so evident in our schools. We even have separate times and separate facilities for training mind and body. A youth in high school is expected to sit quietly in his seat, paying no attention to his peers, and concentrate on his book or the words of his teacher most of the day. Then there is a period when he goes to the playground or gymnasium and jumps around, so that his body also may receive a little training. He does not use his body in the classroom, and presumably has little use for his mind in the gymnasium.

Health has been a stated objective for secondary education for a long time. It was made explicit in 1918 by the publication of the ten cardinal principles of secondary education, and probably long before that. But it has ordinarily been thought of as physical health, while mental health has been ignored or shrouded in mystery. Because health has been considered a matter of the body, we have our gymnasiums and instruction in such matters as diet and exercise. This is all to the good except that it perpetuates the separate mind-body concept, which leads us into many harmful practices.

The whole notion of training rather than educating our young does much damage. We train our dogs and horses. In order to do this, we not only drill them to make the right responses, but the larger part of training is the elimination of responses not wanted by the trainer. These domesticated animals are better off when part of their responses are eliminated, since they live by the sufferance of their owners, and could not survive on their own anyway. Many wild animals are born with instinctive responses which have survival value.

But man is the only truly thinking animal. He has virtually no built-in instincts for survival. Therefore his ability to think—to use his intelligence in working out his survival—is all he has. The ability to think, to use intelligence in the solution of unpredictable problems, is a wonderful instrument. It can be seen that any program which has the automatic elimination of responses at its base really endangers survival. The elimination of responses versus the development of creative thinking brought to bear on ever-evolving new situations is the difference between training and education.

The separation of mind and body has long been abandoned by all students of behavior, and by many medical doctors. One medical doctor I know says that there never was a mental illness without there first being a physical cause, but even he admits that body and mind are not a duality. The recognition of the unified nature of man will finally come to all, and then many of life's problems will be approached differently.* This is the main thesis of *The Next Development in Man* by L. L. Whyte.

The ability and opportunity to think freely about all phases of life is perhaps man's most priceless possession. Its development has to be the primary purpose of education. This is not accomplished by merely reading or listening to the thoughts of others. Education will always be handicapped as long as we cling to the belief in the separation of mind and body; as long as we believe that the mind can and should be trained separately.

10) *Some of the attackers, and many other people, think it is bad to be adjusted.* Whenever the principal of a school says that adjustment to others is one of the objectives of his school, it brings forth loud complaints, even scoffing. They are the champions of the unadjusted. They

* See L. L. Whyte, *The Next Development in Man* (New York: Holt, Rinehart & Winston, Inc., 1948).

say that our youth are being pampered, and they ought to be made to do their work without regard to human relations.

They do not realize that adjustment to other human beings and to novel situations is a requirement for anyone who is to make his way in the world. Nobody can survive in our closely knit society without it. And adjustment has to be learned, just as everything else must be. It cannot be learned in a vacuum—in solitary confinement.

Adjusting to other people and to the situation in which one finds himself is probably the most important learning anyone ever achieves. It is more important than learning science, or mathematics, or grammar, or reading, or making touchdowns. Most of the failures in all walks of life are not due to lack of knowledge, although more knowledge is always desirable, but to the individual's inability to adjust to other people. In spite of the fact that our teachers have been publicized as a pretty stupid lot, those who lose their jobs usually lose them because they cannot get along with their administrators, colleagues and learners, and not because they did not know their subject matter.

Every individual who lives in any community has this problem. No one is born knowing how to adjust to others. It has to be learned. Every person has what on the surface appears to be two conflicting needs. One is his own ego demands—he has to look out for himself. His other need is that he must have other people. There is no other way by which his brain may be developed. No one ever developed into anything that could be called human without other people.

It would seem on the surface that if one has to look out for himself, the simplest way to do it is just to take what he wants, to crush opposition. This is the naïve view beyond which some people never advance. The trouble with this is that such a person will soon be shunned, isolated, and deprived of the very stuff of which his human powers are built.

So perhaps the most basic problem confronting every human being is how he can maintain himself in a way to satisfy his ego and at the same time conduct himself in a manner that will draw other people to him for mutual human development.

"Adjustment" is often attacked by the uninformed critics of education. Nowhere in their writings have I seen mention of attitude, emotion, readiness, maturity, as factors in learning—as though these did not exist. But dealing with such factors is necessarily the main business of the teacher. He cannot escape it no matter how he teaches or how hard he tries. He may of course reject and eject the unadjusted, but this does not solve the problem. It is running away from it. The critics of education who favor maladjustment by opposing adjustment as a desirable objective of education know not what they do. The public acceptance of their ignorance is doing incredible and irreparable harm to our young.

Overlooked by many is the fact that when any person, young or old, gets too far out of adjustment with his associates he is said to be insane. That is what insanity means. It is hardly necessary to point out here that mental illness is increasing at a startling rate. This is particularly true among our youth. Young people are becoming mentally ill in our urban culture at such a rate that our facilities for treatment and care are utterly inadequate. So these youth who we have made ill through deprivation and rejection have to be released to live among us, and often to shift for themselves. Many see all people as enemies, and are bent on the destruction of their fellows. Some become murderers; others turn their hatred against themselves and commit suicide. Yet we debate in our legislatures not on how care can be extended, but how it can be reduced. Our schools are exhorted to step up existing isolating methods.

Sometimes adjustment is attacked on the ground that the well-adjusted person is a conformist, and at this point and at no other the attackers begin to cherish the rebel in us. They imply that one cannot be an individual and adjusted at the same time. They fail to understand how individuals and individuality are built. Modern society has a tendency to promote conformity, to the detriment of humankind. We are exposed to the same lessons, television programs, radio programs, canned goods, frozen whole dinners, and so on. But associating with other people is one of the few things left that is not repetitive, and not the same for all, because people are different. When we learn to behave in such a way that we may have social relationships with others, we come into possession of one of the few things left that is not conforming in its tendency. Of course we have to watch our manners in order to have social relationships with other people, but the cost in individuality thus required is far outweighed by the exposure to ever changing, ever emerging human experience.

11) *All people who are unhappy about our schools think that the school they are against really exists.* This is the so-called "progressive" school, where the children do just as they please and anarchy has been established in the place of authoritarianism.

It has now been about forty years since the founding of the Progressive Education Association. Although John Dewey did not found it, as most people believe, the people who tried to bring many nebulous ideas together to promote them through organization did look to Dewey as their leader. In brief, the idea behind it was to put into practice the use of intelligence in the solution of all human problems, and to give children and youth opportunities to learn this approach to life while they are in school. This called for a problem-solving approach to learning. Indeed, if I were asked to state in one sentence the meaning of the vast works of Dewey, I could do no better than to say that he sought to have all people, young and old, depend on their intelligence to solve the problems of life, and that the decisions resulting from this process would then turn out to be the best available. This is, of course, an attack on the use of ritual, dogma, habit, custom, tradition, voodooism, and all the rest of the bases other than the power to think.

Some people who are unfamiliar with matters concerning learning may say at this point that in all schools youth have problems to solve. In the arithmetic class a child is told the dimensions of an imaginary room and asked to figure how much carpet will be needed to cover the floor, or how much paper the walls will require. Is this not a problem?

It is not a genuine problem because the room is imaginary, its dimensions are dreamed up by someone other than the learner, all of the conditions are set by someone, and the answer has no value except to please someone else. In fact, it is possible in some schools to go all of the way from the kindergarten to the doctor's degree without ever encountering a real problem as part of school work.

The ferment which resulted in the foundation of the Progressive Education Association did not start with Dewey. In many ways the ideas were similar to those of Froebel, Rousseau, and Pestalozzi. Dewey emerged as the twentieth century leader, and his writings crystallized a discontent of many years' standing. I hope no one will think, due to my effort to be brief, that I underestimate Dewey. I regard him as the greatest mind America has so far produced. I am simply trying to express one central idea that he worked to promote. Dewey found the discontent with the unthinking curriculum, and his leadership brought it into some sort of action.

Dissatisfaction with the traditional school is of long standing. A good example of this has been the emergence of certification requirements and institutions of teacher education. There was a time, not too long ago, when all teacher training was in the hands of the so-called arts colleges. There were two main difficulties with this. The first was that the arts colleges did not produce nearly enough teachers to meet even the small needs of fifty years ago, the arts professors being primarily interested in producing experts in their own areas. The second was that teachers so produced were not good teachers. They were for the most part unaware of the human aspects of teaching and learning. Schools and colleges of education came into being through public demand and not, as some attackers hold, through the Machiavellian connivance of people who were power-mad and who wanted to be deans and professors of education. These attackers flatter such people both as to their ability to connive and to wield power.

So the Progressive Education Association was a product of the times. The times called for a more rational education than tradition and mythology had been able to furnish. Its upsurgence coincided with the period when the American public had accepted the idea of education for all, and the old course of study was even less applicable than it had been in the past. It found a great leader who had been advocating the use of intelligence in the solution of human problems since about 1890.

It would seem that this idea would be readily acceptable by all. It seems now, when we have got so far away from it, to be a good idea. But it really called out the hounds from the very beginning. It raised the hackles of all authoritarians, and that is a great many people. It enraged the multitude of people who admire and think they wish to return the "good old days." Nearly every newspaper and magazine editor took up the cry against it. Perhaps most damaging of all, teachers who had been going through the same motions for years saw that this idea called for a change in their methods, and, fearing to change, derided it. Many silly stories were made up and told as though they had really occurred.

Of course any new movement has to bear the burden of attracting some crackpots and malcontents—people who would not be satisfied under any conditions. The Progressive Education Association got its share, or more. And so I presume that many things went on in the name of progressive education which no one in his right mind could support. The whole movement, under attack from the authoritarians and suffering from the deeds of some of its members, came to be misunderstood and misinterpreted. Most of the disdain was heaped on John Dewey, who, in a sense, had been an innocent bystander. In 1938 he wrote a short book in an attempt to make his position clear. It is titled *Experience and Education*. I do not expect the attackers of progressive education to become Dewey scholars. That would take them too long, since they are not students of education. But they could manage to read this little book of Dewey's. If they did so with open minds, they would have a much better idea of Dewey's teachings than they now appear to have.

The idea of the Progressive Education Association never really succeeded in changing our schools from a rote learning base to a problem-solving one. Schools were changed a little, especially in the elementary grades. Whenever teachers' attitudes and beliefs are changed, there is sure to be some modification in behavior. From 1920 to 1957 (Sputnik!) there was a tendency for schools to become more human in their orientation. But even in the elementary schools, most of them never dared depend upon the use of intelligence in the solution of problems, but fell back on rote learning and the reward-punishment concept. This is the main reason why we have so many people who cannot read or cipher. The elementary school people tend to feel superior to the secondary schoolteachers and administrators, but most of the problems which stand in the way of the secondary school doing a better job are created in the elementary school.

There is some effort to make the junior high school a better place for early adolescent boys and girls, but caught between the conditioning of the elementary schools and the subject matter pressure of the senior high schools, they have a most difficult time. There is some effort to establish and operate a core curriculum in the junior high schools. This means an attempt to break down the sharp lines between subjects and do some genuine problem solving. The obstacles to this effort, however, are enormous. Teachers usually do not know how to do this, and many of them do not even have the concepts needed to hear about it. There are some good core programs, of course, but they operate against enormous odds. And so the junior high school, originally created to meet the needs of a particular age group, has retreated from a rational approach to the problems of its students and into a junior copy of the ritualistic senior high school.

The senior high schools were virtually unaffected by the Progressive Education Association. There were perhaps some exceptions, particularly in some private schools. There may have been some teachers who were more humanly oriented. But for the most part, the secondary school has clung tenaciously to the methods used in the nineteenth century, before the time of Dewey. There has been improvement in buildings, in furniture, in teaching materials, in textbooks. Teachers are better educated, better paid, better dressed. The method is, however, basically the same as it was in 1900. This is the assignment, the recitation, the examination, all of which ignores the learner as a rational being. This method is the opposite of the problem-solving process, in which the use of intelligence is relevant.

All of this is to make the point that the school so many people think they are against unfortunately does not really exist, and never has. These people, most people I fear, carry a picture in their heads of a wasteful, purposeless school, where anarchy prevails. This picture does enormous damage to our young. The picture has been created by the attackers, through our newspapers, magazines and television. A long time ago I read a column by Walter Lippmann, American pundit with vast influence, stating that the real trouble with our schools was that they had been ruined by progressive education. Inez Robb, a columnist if not quite a pundit, has more than once mentioned basket weaving, giving the impression that this is a prominent item in the course of study of the high schools. This puzzles me, because there is no basket weaving in our high schools with the possible exception of arts and craft classes, and generally not even in these.* The idea has occurred to me that perhaps Mrs. Robb glanced at the sport page and saw something about a high school student "making baskets" and misinterpreted it. At any rate, Mr. Lippmann, Mrs. Robb, and a host of others could have found out that these charges were untrue by a brief visit to the nearest high school. And so could the American public very easily discover that the school they are against does not exist.

I have devoted a good deal of space to the beliefs people hold which are not so. Most of these beliefs arose in antiquity, and are in the realm of the mystic. They find little support when one studies the nature of the human organism and how it learns. The reason that these beliefs receive so much attention here is that they govern what we do. They constitute the grip of the dead hand of the past, the pre-scientific time, on education. They do incalculable harm to our young, whom we must nurture in order to survive. And the school which must be a good place for youth, since they have no other in society, cannot become a much better place for youth as long as we cling to them.

* Another item in present-day education which upsets Mrs. Robb is driver training. There is ample research to prove that the driver training in our schools saves lives, and that our annual carnage on the highways would be even worse without it. There are many sources of information on this, for those who seek it. One of these is the Traffic Safety Association of Detroit, 1902 Buhl Building, Detroit.

Chapter 14

Our Schools Have Many Faults

So far in Part III I fear I have seemed to defend the schools as they are. I have, however, spent many years criticizing the schools in an effort to make them better places for youth, who really have no other place in our industrial society. It seems odd to get pushed into a position of defending that which for so many years I have sought to change.

The fact is, however, that while the schools have never been suitable places for all American youth, the attackers seek to make them worse than they have been. All of their energy has been in the direction of trying to get teachers to do what they have been doing wrong harder. The critics have demanded that the schools become more punitive, less considerate of the peculiar differences among youth, more determined to drive most of youth out onto urban streets, with nowhere else to go. It becomes a matter of trying to save what we have, rather than defending it.

While the pre-scientific attack has been continuous for centuries, the tempo of these attacks has been stepped up, particularly since the Russians scared the daylights out of us in October 1957. This fear rendered us incapable of rational thought. It seems that the greater the advance of scientific knowledge in the world, the less we want of it in our schools. And so in recent years the condition of youth has become worse. This has to be paid for with shattered lives, in more crimes, more jails, more guards, financial losses of all kinds. The financial cost of allowing just one person to fail to develop into a consumer, and become instead a ward of the state, is enormous, to say nothing of the human loss.

In all fairness, the schools need some defending, even if they are not places which meet the needs of urban youth. They have had a hard time. During the nineteenth century teachers really had the status of servants. In rural districts, they were forced to "board around," and this board and room was the major part of their pay. They had to spend a portion of their time in each home, and some of these homes were unsavory, to say the least. The struggle for decent status in the community has been a long slow one. Today, teachers have greatly improved their position as to salary and respectability, but they have a long way to go before they can boast about their occupation as a salesman or a vice-president might.

Ever since the close of World War I, when America excluded youth from employment by the enactment of youth labor laws, the schools have become increasingly over-crowded. The curriculum did not fit the newcomers. The teachers did not know anything different to do. Salaries were low, buildings were old, teaching materials were few. The depression came, so that there were more youth and less money. As that decade finally wore itself out, war came, with its scarcity of building materials. Some of the youth went to war, but so did many of the teachers. Draft boards did not consider teachers essential to the war effort.

During the late forties and the fifties considerable school building went on, and some of the new buildings are quite beautiful. Salaries have been increased, although it is doubtful that they have kept up with the rising cost of living. Men teachers with families to support still have to find outside jobs to make ends meet. Some of them drive cars to distant cities over weekends, having to hitch-hike back. Some of them drive trucks at night, others even tend bar.

The new buildings should have made more room, but just at the time they were built, the child population exploded, so that while class size may have been slightly reduced, it is still so high that teachers have had little relief. Besides having far more students than anyone can properly teach, they are loaded with clerical work. The antiquated grading system, where daily records have to be kept and endless averaging goes on, as though the final result had meaning, is a constant matter of concern. Then there are many outside activities, such as clubs and P.T.A. meetings. One must always be at his best for the latter, and pretend to remember individuals out of the mass, so that junior's father and mother will not be offended.

Then there are those periods of the year, amounting to fourteen to eighteen weeks, which the public is pleased to refer to as "vacation." In any other occupation, a cessation of employment without pay is called a lay-off. But people have even been known to tell teachers that they are "lucky" to have all that vacation. Vacation means that the "lucky" ones have to get out and find other jobs, so that they can eat. These jobs are often most menial, and most difficult for anyone who is not accustomed to them.

To face up to this relatively thankless task morning after morning, year after year, is simply heroic. A good many people take the attitude that teachers do this because they are incompetent to do anything else. This is true of some, but I have known thousands of teachers, and the vast majority teach because they want to and have a purpose in life. They are idealistic in that they want the world to be a little better because of them. Some have peculiar ways of showing this after they get into the classroom, but so great is their faith in their ritual that they see themselves as offering something valuable to the cause of humanity.

And so, if I appear to defend our schools as they are, it is not because I think they present a program which will improve the condition of youth. It is because I think they have really "had it." Their burdens are too heavy, their rewards too light. One wonders what our schools might be like today if our teachers had had as much help as they have had hindrance. There has been enough spent in vilification to have made considerable difference if it had been spent to help teachers see their problems as human ones.

We will not get very far, however, in the solution of the problems of urban youth as long as teachers put blind faith in the rituals of what they call their course of study. I will not list these problems, because they are similar to those in the previous chapter. They hold too many beliefs that come down from pre-scientific times, and they do not know, or do not want to know, what research has revealed about learning. Some of the faults of our schools can be summed up briefly.

1) They are not warm and friendly to all kinds of youth. They repel the very ones who need them most.

2) They provide little or no problem-solving situations, where unique creativeness can be practiced and learned.

3) Since what youth are given to do is adult-selected and adult-evaluated, the schools do not teach involvement with its attendant responsibility.

4) They try to teach only that which is not controversial. When anything passes the point of being controversial, it no longer matters, except as history. This keeps both teachers and learners pawing over material that has lost its significance.

5) They are too much in the grip of the dead hand of the past, while youth are naturally looking ahead to decades their elders scarcely dream of.

This list could be longer, but at the risk of being repetitive of what has gone before. There is nothing new here to those who have studied human learning, growing, and motivation. Many before me have said them. So deeply are habit and custom rooted in the past, however, that the practices in schools are among the most resistant to change. We who have labored long to modify the curriculum cannot avoid a certain amount of amusement at the "task forces" and the "crash programs" proposed by the people who have just got around to being horrified by our schools.

Some teachers have become discontented with the futility of pawing over the same pile year after year and have tried to introduce problem-solving research and creativity into their teaching. Some who have a good deal of status have succeeded and proved the practicality of new ways of studying and learning. Too often, though, such teachers have been ostracized by their colleagues, threatened by the parents of their learners, and received "a good talking to" by their administrators. The easiest thing to do, then, is to get back into the same old rut. Pioneering in education is more difficult than it was in the wilderness.

The schools have a long way to go, and many changes in beliefs and practices will be required before they can become the institution which is required if we are to nourish our young.

Chapter 15

Research Tells Us Many Things

I have spent a good deal of time setting forth the beliefs held by teachers and laymen which have no validity in any research. They come to us out of the dim past when people were controlled by their fears. These were the days of great religious intolerance, of mysticism and of witchcraft. Beliefs are what control action and establish what our schools are to be like. It has been said that the American people would rather believe than to know. As long as we cling to these pre-scientific beliefs, we will be doing the wrong things to or for our young. If we do anything right, it will be by mere chance. This will cause us infinite trouble, alienating our most cherished possession.

The alternative to holding untenable and unsupportable beliefs is to look to the findings of science. Many competent scientists have spent much time in the study of the nature of our young, and therefore there is a rich store of information available to us so that we do not need to operate with false concepts. A concept is apt to be false if it has not been or cannot be supported by research.

The scientific method is the best way so far discovered for getting information on which one may act with some confidence. I do not speak of the scientific method in a narrow sense. Some may think of science as what occurs in a laboratory. But the scientific method is a way of life and is quite as apropos to the social studies, for example, as it is to the physics laboratory. In fact, if one does not encounter the scientific way of thinking until he reaches the physics laboratory, it will be difficult for him to acquire it all at once. The scientific way of life is the way, and the only way I know of, to avoid superstition, prejudice and mysticism.

One who would proceed scientifically simply looks to nature to see what it is like before deciding what to do or how to do it. Then he goes ahead in as logical a way as possible to accomplish his objective. I use the word "nature" here because I want a broad term which will include people, animals, plants, inanimate objects (things). It will be seen that this can occur any time, in any pursuit, not just in a laboratory.

The opposite way of doing is called animism. Simply stated, this means investing the inanimate with life or purpose. Formerly, we said that an object which interfered with us was possessed of devils. We all do this in some degree We speak of the perversity of inanimate objects—the scissors won't cut, the cobblestone trips, one hits his thumb with a hammer and curses the hammer—giving powers or evil spirits to things which could not possibly have them.

An historical example of the scientific method versus animism will illustrate this point. In the early part of the seventeenth century, Galileo said that a light object would fall at the same rate as a heavy one. The wise men of his day said that this was ridiculous, that everybody knew that a heavy object would obviously fall faster than a light one. Galileo then proposed that they try an experiment. He took two balls, one heavy and one light, and dropped them together. They hit the ground at the same time. In other words, instead of depending on past opinion, he looked to nature; he tried it out.

The wise men, however, said that this proved nothing, that the balls must be possessed of devils; thus animating the balls to account for their behavior. The scientific method applied to education calls for us to look to the child, or the learner, to see what he is like before deciding how he can be educated. The findings of research can help us to do this. We indulge in animism, or unscientific procedure (one cannot say method) when we say that our young are perverse, possessed of devils, and have to be coerced, broken, and trained. We are animistic when we look to the subject, be it mathematics, foreign language, or any other, and endow it with magic powers, considering it to be educative in itself. Too many people believe that inanimate subject matter is possessed of powers inherent in it so that if the subject matter can be forced into the learner, he will magically become educated. The learner is what is to be educated, and we need to look to him to see what he is like. By this procedure many of the problems of education could be solved, and we would be free from the heavy hand of prejudice, superstition, and mysticism.

Looking to the learner to see how he learns and hence may be educated is a relatively new idea. It was not done by many until after 1900. Children were to be seen and not heard. They were not really considered to be people. So new is this idea that it is not common even now, especially in the secondary schools. The secondary schools cannot be good places for youth until we begin to look scientifically to their needs and stop investing books with magical powers.

I shall now list some of the findings of science related to the nature of the human organism and how it learns. This list should be considered only a sample. There is so much known in this area that to attempt to do a thorough piece of work on it would require many volumes. It is possible, however, to give some central ideas briefly which if accepted and acted upon would make an enormous difference in the quality of living in our schools. These alone would add greatly to the amount of learning, greatly increase the amount of subject matter taken in by our learners. It must be repeated here that we want and need far more learning of subject matter than is now achieved and that our animistic beliefs inhibit learning rather than promoting it.

1) The quality of human inheritance has been unchanged since the dawn of human history. Anthropologists say that their research indicates that the earliest men, living before tools or fire were used, had as much capacity for intellectual development as modern man.

There are two quite different kinds of tissue in the human body. One has to do with the maintenance of the present organism in all its complicated operation. It is made up of cells, bone, muscle, skin, nerves, and so on. It is called somatoplasm, and by volume comprises nearly all of the organism. It is mortal.

The other kind of tissue has to do with reproduction, with passing along the characteristics of the species from generation to generation. It is called germ plasm. This germ plasm survives and is the basis for the formation of the new organism. It is thus handed down from adult to young in its precise living form. It is immortal, at least as long as the human species survives.

Nature has invented another remarkable device. Immediately after conception, at which time the beginning of the new individual is formed, when the egg cell and the sperm cell unite, the new combined cell is sealed off so that it has no connection with the mother except for nutrition. This serves the purpose of protecting the new individual from any influence which may affect the mother. It may of course suffer from poor nutrition if the mother cannot supply this need, but it cannot be damaged or changed by such things as neurosis or low cultural standards. The biological inheritance is preserved so that it can be handed down intact again and again.

If this scientific fact were understood and accepted, we would no longer hear the statement that our youth are less able and more perverse than they used to be. This is, I fear, a commonly held belief even by teachers. One of the major contentions of this book is that our young are all right when we get them, and if they are not all right now, it is because of the lives they have lived in an adult-managed world. It is easy to dodge adult responsibility by simply saying that our young are not any good any more. This is a form of animism; adults come very close to saying that our youth are possessed of devils, or at least that they are naturally perverse. When we understand the slowness of the process of evolution; that there has been little or no change since the dawn of history; that provision has been made to protect the newly conceived individual from outside influences, it makes those who claim that the deterioration has occurred since *they* were young seem ridiculous. If we could all be freed from the idea that our youth are basically inferior, it would liberate us to think anew about the nurture of our young.

2) We build and are built by our environment. Perhaps I have already said enough about this. I have called attention to the Iowa studies which showed nearly thirty years ago that rich environments improve intelligence and starved environments reduce it. This is extremely important because it means that a person is not necessarily condemned to be backward all his life. As Howard Lane says, dullness is therefore more an achievement than a gift.

Another great research work which is more recent is that of Ames in the area of perception. From this work we can understand how it is possible for man to build and be built by his environment. Since everything that feeds the psychological self comes to the individual through perception, this becomes the crucial phenomenon in learning, attitude, emotion or value.*

Many people seem not to realize that in providing an environment, such as a classroom, for youth, we are in fact building people, and they will become that which is built. These people seem to think that it is good for us to set up a rigid environment and demand that the learner make the best of it. Although they are opposed to adjustment, they expect youth to adjust to what they provide with no questions asked.

They do not seem to realize that a hostile environment builds hostility, aggression begets aggression; the response to hate is hate. And so they are surprised, sad, and blameful when our youth leave a hostile, aggressive and hateful environment and behave in society as hostile people. They do not realize that if we are to produce loving, peaceful people, we must provide a loving, peaceful environment.

3) Each human being in the world is unique; that is, he is significantly different from every other person in the whole world. It does not require

* It will not be possible here to describe Ames' works in any detail. For those who want verification, I refer you to Earl C. Kelley, *Education for What Is Real* (New York: Harper & Brothers, 1947). For a more complete statement on man's relationship to his environment, see Kelley and Rasey, *Education and the Nature of Man* (New York: Harper & Brothers, 1952).

a scientist to see that no two people look alike and to say glibly that "people are different." But science has produced the reasons why no two people can be the same. For a long time we have known how, in cell structure, one person is made from two in such a way that duplication is so nearly impossible that the chance of it can be ignored. This means that no two persons (including identical twins) can start life with the same biological equipment. This accounts for the fact that physically no two people look alike, although they may resemble either or both parents. It probably accounts, too, for a good deal more than just physical characteristics, such as unique purpose.*

This is only part of the story of uniqueness. Ames has shown us that the psychological self, which controls behavior, is built and nurtured by the perceptive process and that perception is highly selective. No person can possibly perceive all that is about him, and each unconsciously or automatically selects out of any environment that which he will perceive. This is done on the basis of one's experience and purpose. Since no two people can have the same background of experience, no two people can perceive the same or build the same psychological self.

The significance of being unique, the explanation of which research makes so clear, is one of the central facts of life. It is any person's reason for being. It means that every person in the world has something which nobody else has. So he is, in a sense, indispensable. Whenever anyone dies, something special to him goes and cannot be replaced. If people were not unique, one person would serve just as well as another. It is therefore our differences which make us valuable.

If our teachers really knew and believed what research has told us about uniqueness, it would make a great deal of difference in our school programs. Of course, recognizing that every learner is unique in what he can or will learn would cause difficulties. But it really is nobody's fault that children are not all alike. It is just a fact of life. We do hear a good deal of talk about individual differences, but we do not see much modification of program to provide for this fact. They too frequently depend upon the same textbook and assignment for all, and expect the same achievement for all. It almost seems as though they expected to iron out the learners' uniqueness and bring them through without any, in spite of the way nature made them.

Of course, this flight from reality on the part of teachers becomes almost a necessity in the face of the demand for uniformity, conformity, and rigidity on the part of our newspapers, magazines, and self-appointed

* See Erwin Schroedinger's book (91 pages) *What is Life?* (New York: The Macmillan Company, 1945).

experts. The American citizens make it almost impossible for teachers to nurture differences when they provide so little room, pack so many of their own into small classrooms, that it becomes increasingly difficult for the teacher to do anything except to teach everyone alike. The newspaper and magazine editors, the self-appointed experts, the penny wise, pound foolish citizens do not comprehend the significance of being unique or what it takes to nurture uniqueness. They do not understand the danger of conformity or the forces of nature against which they contend when they cry out for the abolition of human uniqueness. They do not know what science has revealed concerning the human organism and are operating on untenable beliefs handed down from the pre-scientific era.

4) Every living thing possesses the dynamic of growth. Taken superficially I suppose nobody would dispute this. Teachers and parents see their children getting bigger each year and are concerned when a child does not do this. Research has revealed, however, that physical growth is only part of the story. Physical growth is temporary, ceasing with adulthood.

The growth which is little understood is that of the psychological self. It is fed by the process of perception. It goes on continuously throughout life; it does not cease when one becomes an adult. The teacher, therefore, is providing the stuff day by day out of which the functioning person is built and opening or closing the perceptive avenues through which the stuff of growth must come.

An understanding of the nature of the growth of personality, the psychological self, would modify many of the practices of education. We would not longer expect the growing individual to take in what his perceptive process cannot receive, any more than we would expect anyone to take in a food which nauseates him and causes him to throw it off. We would see that hostility builds hostile people, that being the stuff for psychological growth which is available to them. We would see that if a person is to build a courageous self he will need courage rather than fear to build it with.

5) Maturation is a scientific fact which must be taken into account. Since the individual starts as a single cell with nothing but potentialities and grows until death, there is a point where it cannot comprehend anything, and the ability to comprehend is a gradual process, differing in each individual because he is unique. The ability to do abstract thinking is a highly developed mental process and comes later than the ability to comprehend concrete things. In some people the ability to think in the abstract never develops very much. It is not known whether or not these people could have, in the proper environment, developed this

ability, but what is known about learning would indicate that they could.

The people with little talent for abstraction are not bad people or useless people, but they will spend their lives differently and make different contributions from those more able to abstract. This does not mean that these non-abstracting people will be the "hewers of wood and drawers of water." Some of the highest reaches of human endeavor are open to them; indeed, they often seem to excel in them. These often seem to be the people who can offer the milk of human kindness to all mankind. Where does the influence of such people end? The total effect of a good nurse, a good homemaker, a loving teacher is apt to be even greater in human terms than that of a good statistician or physicist.

The fact of unique maturation is so obvious that it would seem to be a waste of time to belabor it. Nobody would expect a newborn babe to learn trigonometry. But we forget this obvious fact when a child becomes six years old. Then he has to learn to read, ready or not. Reading is a process of abstraction by which marks on paper are translated into language. At age seven, everyone is expected to learn and understand the beginnings of mathematics. Besides, we often start with the short-hand for quantitative thinking: e.g., $7 + 5 = 12$ is short-hand.

If the unique learner has not grown by this time to the point where it is possible to abstract to this degree, we begin to bring pressure to bear upon him. He is eventually subjected to failure for not doing what he has not developed maturity to do, and to the opprobrium of his parents and his peers. He may even be moved into a whole class of non-abstracting people to be "remedied."

It has been known for a long time that children vary in their ability to learn to read. Some can do it at age three, others not until age ten or twelve. Some have learned all that is contained in the elementary mathematics curriculum in one semester after they have gained the maturation to comprehend it. But because of pre-scientific notions we still insist that they are all ready at the same time, and we invest with devils those who are not. Of course, a child should be taught to read and cipher as soon as he can, because these are fine tools to have. But we simply must bide our time without rejection if we are to use our intelligence instead of our mythology in the solution of this problem.

Some may wonder what all this has to do with the school as a good place for youth. It has important bearing, because many rebels against society are made at this point. Some of these become our delinquents, preying on a society which has rejected them for not doing what they could not do.

6) The human organism works as a whole, not in parts. A person is made up of a physical body and a psychological self so inter-related as to be inseparable. Functionally, an attitude is as much a part of structure as a hand. The portion of a person we see is only a part of the total person. Whenever anyone does anything in relation to another, he needs to take this into account. This is so well known that it hardly needs any argument. There are not many medical doctors left who think they can treat physical symptoms alone without regard to the patient's attitude, emotion, fear, and so on. We do not know as much about the closeness of this relationship as we will eventually, but we know a great deal about it. Some scholars in this area say that they should not be surprised if we discover that all physical illness has its base in the psychological structure.

As well known as the fact of the wholeness of the individual is, the idea seems to have made little progress in our schools, especially the secondary schools, which need to be a good place for our youth. It is our secondary school age group mainly who are large enough to make war on our society, or to serve it. Many of the critics of our schools proclaim that the school is a place to train the mind and that the attitudes, feelings, or beliefs of our youth have nothing to do with it. It is said that our youth ought to learn their attitudes and values at home and their subject matter at school. Further, if we have to take responsibility for attitude and emotion as well as arithmetic, they say we just cannot afford it.

It is beside the point whether we like this scientific finding or not. It just happens to be so, as truly as we know that water is composed of oxygen and hydrogen. Growth, for weal or woe, is continuous; attitudes which are being formed while we teach our subject matter cannot be suspended. What "ought" to be has nothing to do with the matter at all. Our homes teach attitudes too, whether intentionally or otherwise. Life would be much simpler if our young could learn their values at home and their subject matter at school; but that is not the way it is, and as long as we ignore this fact, we will continue to have a good many youth who are hostile to us.

7) Human beings yearn for some contact with the earth from which we all sprang. Although this is not proven by research, there is overwhelming evidence from observation that this is true. We may be able in the future to document it in the same way that other scientific facts are proven.

If this is a great human need, as I firmly believe it to be, it has many implications for city schools. This need has been recognized by many.

Schools in many sections of America have attempted to meet this need by conducting programs in outdoor education. They do this by taking groups of children or youth to a campsite in the country for a period of co-operative camp living. We now have a great deal of information concerning the effectiveness of these programs. Due to hysteria caused by the attackers and the reduction in financial support which has followed, many of the school districts which have had programs in outdoor education have had to eliminate them. This little peek at the earth and sky has been attacked on the ground that it is a frill, and in many cases has been denied our young.

A great and rather undefinable value in outdoor education is that the city youth gets an opportunity to relate to the earth and sky. City youth seldom see anything that is not man-made. Sidewalks, curbs, streets, buildings are all in straight lines, but nature never uses a straight line. Even the parks are laid out and planted according to man's notion of what nature might devise. Research does not reveal what it is that causes man's spirit to expand when he comes in contact with the earth from which he sprang.

No one who has ever seen a sunset or felt the warm earth of spring under his feet can deny that something enhancing to human development exists here. This is doubtless the reason the deer hunter, the trout fisherman, or the bird shooter gets a wild look in his eye at certain times of the year and hies himself to the woods. He does this at enormous cost to himself in money and discomfort. He eats food he would not touch at home, sleeps under conditions he would ordinarily consider torture. It is not for meat that he does this, although he may stoutly deny this statement. "Progress" has long since settled this matter for all of us. Modern man can get better meat and more of it for the money within a few blocks of his home. It is rather the call to nature and to the earth that spurs him on. And he is glad—counts it worthwhile—even though he brings home no game and is pained in body and in purse. He has satisfied a yearning beyond pain.

So it is with the city youth. We have observed personality changes for the better when city youth encounter and commune with the earth. There is no substitute for this in the city situation. Many thousands of our city youth never get the opportunity to know what communing with nature means. Some time research may be able to tell us more about what happens when one gets an opportunity to relate himself to his earth, but that changes do occur seems indisputable.

Outdoor education in a camp setting need not be as expensive as it appears at first glance. Many school plants are now being built. Part of the plant could be at a nearby place where woods and water are available. We have to begin to think of the school as serving the needs of youth before we can see a different school plant. With planning, both in building and in curriculum, the program could be devised so that the campsite is an integral part of the school system. The outdoor program, then, would be carried on with the camp operating as just another part of the school plant.

I see outdoor education as significant because it is a part of the curriculum.

It takes place on school time. It provides opportunity for returning something to children that has been taken away by urbanization. It is in keeping with modern research on the nature of the human organism and of learning. It gives some opportunity for city children to see the earth, to live cooperatively and democratically and to learn to assume responsibility. It even provides an opportunity to live creatively for a time. And I believe that creative living is the best way to learn how to be a part of a changing world.*

These are some of the facts about the nature of the human organism which are known to science and which must, therefore, be taken into account when learning is to be brought about. The list could be much expanded and amplified, but this would tend to confuse rather than to clarify. If just this much of the findings of science were known and used, it would modify our schools to such an extent that we would hardly recognize them as what we now call schools. To do this we would have to abandon our animism, and our schools would become good places for our young to grow.

* The quoted material above was written by me in 1957 and is taken from *Outdoor Education and American Youth,* Julian W. Smith, editor, American Association for Health, Physical Education, and Recreation, Washington, D. C., 1957.

Chapter 16

What Are the Fundamentals?

If we are to look upon education as building whole people so that they can function in a democratic society, we must re-examine what is fundamental. I suppose if we were to ask almost anyone what the fundamentals are, he would cite the three R's, meaning reading, writing and ciphering. This is in keeping with the notion that the school is the place for book learning, that the rest of the organism does not and should not grow in school but should do it somewhere else.

With a scientific approach to education we obviously need a new definition of what is fundamental. It seems to me that *anything is fundamental without which the organism cannot thrive.* I do not say "cannot live," because organisms of all sorts are extremely tenacious of life. Just being alive means very little when compared to becoming a thriving, adequate human being. In fact, there are people who never developed any psychological selves, others who through brain damage have lost what they had, but who live on in a physical sense.

With this definition we can see that the so-called three R's are not fundamental. This has to be granted because we know so many people who have thrived without one or all of them. There are many fine human beings in the world who do not have them. For example, a large percentage of our population, including many college graduates, have almost no skill in mathematics. These people are considered successful because they have lived well. They often have raised fine families, met economic obligations, extended love to many people.

The three R's are skills which facilitate living in our present society. They are, of course, desirable, and we should teach them as much and as well as we can, but they are not necessarily essential to the good life, and we should not teach them so insistently and so aggressively that we diminish the individual's ability to grow toward humanness.

Following is a list of six things which seem to be essential if the human organism is to thrive. The list could doubtless be extended. Since some of these must and do come at the same time, it is difficult to establish a proper order for them. Some have to be provided in early infancy, but all are continuously essential through life and must therefore be provided by the school for that time when the school is a prominent part of life.

1) The first fundamental is other people. The infant is born with the equipment for becoming human. Nature provides that no human being shall be deprived of at least one other person. The human infant is born completely helpless and has to be cared for by another human being, usually its mother, if it is to survive. Its undeveloped cortex can be built in no other way. This is the meaning of the long infancy in the human species. The lower animals are, at least in most cases, not so dependent on their mothers. They do not need this cortical development because they have little or no cortex and in many instances are able to fend for themselves immediately. The baby chick, for example, can start pecking for its food almost as soon as it is out of the shell. In fact, it comes equipped with the instinct to peck. The lower animals seem to come into life with a good many instincts so that they can survive without assistance. The human infant comes equipped with almost no instincts at all, seemingly to compel others to provide for it. Thus nature provides another person for the beginning of life at least. This need is continuous throughout life, because the human potentiality for psychological growth is continuous.

2) In order to have other people we need good *communication* between at least one adult and the very young. This seems self-evident, but the whole business of communication is more complicated than has ordinarily been supposed. The way in which the mother communicates with the babe and in which other adults do so is of greatest importance. Communication is not a one-way affair. Too often it has been believed that just to send messages constituted communication. For example, the radio and television experts call themselves communications people, but all they do is broadcast, and they may have no receivers at all. Teachers often labor under the delusion that to send, to lecture, to tell, is to communicate. There never is any communication until what is sent has been received, and the condition of the receiver is more important than what is sent.

All of us, beginning at birth and throughout life, look out upon our surroundings to see whether those about us seem likely to help or threaten us. When the human environment looks facilitating we tend to open up and to be receptive, that is, more accessible to communications. If the human environment seems threatening, we tend to withdraw, to build barriers for our protection. We become less receptive, less accessible. Sometimes in early infancy the avenues of communication become entirely closed, and such children are then called autistic. These children, due to their view of their world, have cut off all communication, and they become mere physical organisms. This is what can happen under extremely adverse circumstances. There are all degrees of communication, from the autistic to the open self. The establishment of facilitating communication is certainly one of the fundamentals without which no organism can thrive.

3) In order to establish communication, to have other people, the human being must have other people in a *loving relationship*. If he is to develop into a person who can maintain human relationship, he must be a loving person. By some strange device nature has arranged for mother love which often "passeth all understanding." Of course, this does not always apply, because the mother sometimes has been damaged psychologically and may be so neurotic as to reject her own offspring. Ordinarily, however, this is not the case, and in normal instances love is automatically provided at the start of life.

If the infant is for some reason denied love in the beginning, he builds not love but hostility. This leads to isolation and deprivation of the stuff out of which adequate humans are built. This stuff, of course, is other people, and those who are driven into isolation are deprived of that which they must have if they are to be really human.

Some may be bothered by the use of the word "love" in this regard. Perhaps this is because the word has been used in a romantic sense for so long. This is only one of many meanings given in dictionaries. It is the only word strong enough to express the acceptance needed between two human beings, or among all, for the proper development of human personality. This is the meaning of the admonition "Thou shalt love thy neighbor as thyself," (Matthew 22:39). Ashley Montagu, anthropologist, writes mainly about the fundamental essential of love in a book which should be read by all who think that we should "get tough" with our own young.*

Christ was not the only religious leader who advocated love among humans as essential to the good life. This has been done by religious leaders, poets and seers for centuries. Christ's words came many centuries before it was known that man even had a cortex, much less how it had to be developed. It is curious how scientific study has repeatedly verified (or found base for) these great teachings.** It is curious, too,

* Ashley Montagu, *Education and Human Relations* (New York: Grove Press, Inc., 1958).

** Cantril and Bumstead present a whole volume of evidence on this point in their *Reflections on the Human Venture* (New York: New York University Press, 1960).

how some people can attend churches and synagogues on the sabbath to hear about the importance of love in human relationships and then contend that love is not needed by youth, that what they need is coercion; that those who do not yield to coercion should then be rejected.*

4) A fourth fundamental is that each person must have a *workable concept of self.* The word "workable" is used here after some thought and searching. One needs to think well enough of himself so that he can operate. Perhaps none of us escapes the rigors of life without some damage to our concepts of our own selves. Abraham Maslow describes those who he thinks have not been damaged as "self-actualizing" but says he can name only a very few. So conceding that almost no one is going to develop unscathed in this regard, we still must have people who think well enough of themselves so that they can face the vicissitudes of life. When a person does not think well of himself, he is crippled and cannot do anything. Nobody can do anything unless he thinks he can.

This may seem at first to support the show-off, the egotist. But such a person behaves in this way because he feels his inadequacy keenly and is trying to cover up by aggressive action. He comes as far from the mark of good human relations as do those who withdraw.

Workable concepts of self are built by the life good to live, in full love and acceptance of one's fellows. The unloved and unwanted become crippled and cannot thrive.

5) Every human being, in order to develop his full potential, must have *freedom.* This requirement is evidently built into the organism. The effort humans have made to achieve freedom is well known from studies of the history of man from the very beginning. While many people have lived and died in various forms of slavery, the masters have always had to be repressive and have lived in fear that the spirits of those they oppressed would break out in reprisal.

This great need is grossly misunderstood by many. It does not mean that anybody in these times has the right to do just as he pleases. The very fact of our living so closely together naturally limits this right. The right to do just as he pleases could only be achieved by a hermit. But one of the fundamentals is the need for other people. In order to have other people the individual must behave in such a way that, while he has the choices of a free man, other people will not be repelled. This is

* Laymen who want to understand better the fundamental need of love in school will profit from reading Lane and Beauchamp, *Human Relations in Teaching* (Englewood Cliffs, N. J.: Prentice Hall, Inc., 1955), and their *Understanding Human Development* (Englewood Cliffs, N. J.: Prentice Hall, Inc., 1959). Also see Lawrence K. Frank, *The Fundamental Needs of the Child* (New York: New York Committee on Mental Hygiene, 1937).

freedom within the social scene. It is the product of cooperative living.

In order to live so that one can have the benefit of other people he has to surrender certain minor freedoms. Whenever one surrenders minor freedoms he is able to achieve freedom on a higher level. For example, I am not permitted to leave the street in front of my house unpaved. But neither may anyone else do this, so that we do not have spaces in our streets which are not paved. Having given up that freedom, I achieve the freedom of driving along streets without being stopped by mud holes which might exist if everyone was free to decide for himself.

There is enough freedom within the social scene—within cooperative living—to provide for making choices. We do not have to accept either autocracy or anarchy. While the need for freedom seems to be present in all humans, the capacity to exercise it within the social scene has to be learned. It can be learned in an atmosphere of love, democracy, cooperation.

6) Every person needs the chance to be *creative*. This does not mean that everyone should paint a picture or write a symphony. Creativity occurs whenever a person contrives a new way out of a unique dilemma. It is simply meeting the problems of living and inventing new ways to solve them. Most of us do this every day in a greater or lesser degree. Creativity is the growing edge of learning and living and is essential to any real life fulfillment. It can only take place in an atmosphere of freedom. In fact, freedom begets creativity; that is, when one is free he will naturally contrive. When he contrives he is fulfilled. When he is fulfilled he may be said to thrive.

Here then are the fundamentals, at least in part. There probably are others, but these are the ones which occur to me. If our youth have these, they will thrive.

To those who still cling to the three R's as fundamental, I would say that the three R's are tools good to have, but that they never alone saved a boy from becoming delinquent. The most urgent needs of our youth go much deeper than the three R's. Indeed, the three R's cannot even be learned at all unless at least part of the above fundamentals are met. Some of these needs have to be met in infancy, and there is little the school can do about them except to rear a generation of people who will not reject their own young. But most of these needs are continuous throughout life and can be provided by the school.

We will never solve the problem of the three R's, which seems to vex so many people, until we learn to live with our young in such a way that they can be open to receive such matters.

Chapter 17

Conclusion

It has been nearly two years since the first words of this book were written. I had hoped to finish it in much less time, since I felt that our youth were being allowed to deteriorate, and I was filled with a feeling of urgency. I assigned myself this task because what I was reading and hearing about youth did not square with my experience and knowledge concerning young people. As I have spent my entire adult life either with youth or working for their cause, it seemed a matter of conscience that I attempt to set forth a statement concerning them. I believe it was Mark Twain who said "If I had a yaller dog as mean as my conscience I'd pizen him."

Two years ago I was disturbed—indeed frightened—by the attitudes displayed by adults toward their own progeny, and by many youth who seem to be delinquent, to be mentally ill, and to be antagonistic toward their own parents, their teachers, law enforcement officials, and toward adults in general. Many of them seemed alienated from self and others. I was alarmed by the fact that most adults thought the solution was more coercion, in the face of the fact that coercive measures had brought us to our sad state. It seemed clear that what our youth had to have was more acceptance, more love, and a better chance to learn the co-operative way of life; that if we continued to hold that more coercion and rejection were what was needed, the condition of youth could only get worse. Having myself tried coercion, and having been almost forced to try cooperation; having seen the startling success of doing things with youth rather than to them, it seemed the least I could do was to make this record.

I wish that I could say that we have improved during the past two years in our attitudes and treatment of youth, and that my feeling of urgency has subsided. Of this there seems to be no evidence. Locally we are now going through another youth crime wave. Evidence of mental illness is just as abundant as it was two years ago. Millions of children and youth are on part-time schedules in school. We have some new school buildings standing empty because the people refuse to employ staff for them after having built them. The attackers who were so vitriolic two years ago seem to have quieted down somewhat, but we feel sure that another crop will soon emerge.

I believe that the schools, their staffs being frightened by the attackers, and being under heavy pressure from the colleges and universities, are even worse than they were. They have invented new forms of rejection. The people who work in the colleges and universities seem to be concerned not at all for the welfare of American youth, but only for their own convenience.

What is happening in our high schools in the area of testing is a good example of our worsening attitudes in the past two years. The use of standardized tests is growing rapidly, and reaching an alarming volume. There are states using state-wide standardized tests, and some dream of a national curriculum with a national test. Nobody knows how much of our young people's time is used this way, but I have heard estimates that in some schools it is as high as twenty-five per cent.

I speak of excess testing only as one example of the rejection of youth. I do not mean to say that a test should never be used, but tests are often used to obtain grounds for rejection. In fact, they are sometimes used with the hope that the student will fail, so that he may be rejected. Tests provide the means of separating the sheep from the goats, of establishing and recruiting the educationally disinherited. They are usually based purely on one's ability to remember so-called facts, and nothing else. When the staff of a school feels it needs to devote a large percentage of its time, not to learning, but to finding out what is remembered, the teachers and administrators of that school are either frightened or misunderstand their social function. Usually the test is made up by someone far away, for commercial reasons, and the results are sent to someone else far away. Judgments are made about unique human beings in this manner. Rejection thus can come from afar, quite unrelated to anything the youth sees as relevant to him.

The test also has the effect of becoming the curriculum. If a teacher knows that his students are going to be subjected to certain tests, he teaches for the test, and so that which is "thought up" far away becomes the course of study. The chance to explore the field of human knowledge, to be creative, is lost. Freedom of the mind, freedom to know, is thus abrogated.

The central idea of this book is "We must stop rejecting our young. To continue to do so will destroy us." Excessive testing is one of the most highly developed forms of rejection that has so far been invented. The schools are clearly worse in this regard than they were two years ago.

We see many attempts to mechanize education, partly to save money, partly because we still cling to outmoded notions of the nature of knowledge and of learning. One of these is the teaching machines. These devices are based on the old stimulus-response psychology, and I would have said two years ago that no responsible person would turn the clock back that far. I would have been wrong. The usual teaching machine sets up a guessing game in which the student guesses what the person who "fed" the machine thinks is right. If he guesses well, he is rewarded. If not, he is punished. Often it is really a multiple choice test, and belongs not with the teaching part of the day, but must be added to the testing part. Exploration of new frontiers of knowledge for the learner is even more completely excluded than in the older methods of teaching.

One of the great virtues claimed for the teaching (testing) machine is that it is "do it yourself" education, and therefore does not cost anything after the machine is paid for and loaded with answers. The learner goes into an isolation booth, cut off not only from other sources for learning but from all other human beings, and just "learns." While he is doing this, nobody has to pay a teacher for him. Big Brother takes care of everything.

We are going to have to go through this, and it is going to cost us plenty, not only in money for the over-priced machines, but in human resources. But I predict that it will not work, because it is contrary to the true nature of the human organism, of learning and of knowledge. I predict that ten years from now there will be many millions of dollars worth of these machines gathering dust in the basements of the schools of America. Instead of gaining in our frenetic efforts to get knowledge inside the skins of our young and do it at wholesale prices, we shall lose. We shall lose money and young people.

Another way by which we are attempting to buy our education wholesale is the use of television as a large part of the curriculum. Television can be useful in a limited way if we use it for what it can do. But the notion that five hundred young people or children can sit in an auditorium, look at a screen, and become educated is naïve. It will not work. It is clearly based on the notion that education consists of getting subject matter into the organism by what ever means possible. It ignores uniqueness, readiness, purpose, disparity of human circumstance, emotion, attitude. It will fail because it provides no possibility of choices for creativeness, for exploration. Many of the very people who talk about how we must recognize individual differences also support teaching by television!

At this very moment an airplane is flying overhead broadcasting lessons by television, so that every child in southern Michigan, northern Ohio, Indiana, and Illinois can have the very same lesson at the very same time. Knowledge is falling upon us from heaven! This intellectual crop-dusting is falling, like rain, on the just and the unjust alike. Or, more to the point, on the bright and the dull, the lame, the near-deaf, the near-blind, the sick, and the hale. If it is continued and spread, it can become the final triumph of the machine in its tendency to control its own creator. It can be the last word in the establishment of conformity, the death blow to individuality.

Some say "Take it easy! Let's do it and evaluate it." This I suppose we shall have to do, but it will cost many children and youth their chance for creative education. It seems to me to be enormously expensive in terms of human growth. Besides, all of the evaluations of educational television which I have seen compare it to the traditional academic program, which has failed to minister to the needs of so many of our youth. Finding that educational television is as good or slightly better than a program which has already failed to meet our needs is hardly convincing.

I believe that the real hope of those who are literally forcing us into educational television is that it will be cheaper in money. I believe this to be true because if it is not so, their statements become too contradictory for me to credit them. It is a way by which it is hoped that the problem of the crowded classroom can be met. We will do anything, it seems, to avoid paying for a good education for our own.

I have heard people who are earnest, good friends of youth say that we simply cannot afford the burden of good schools. This is nonsense. The people of the richest country in the world buy what they want. It is only a question as to what they value. I believe that we in education should not concede that the American people cannot afford a well educated teacher and an attractive classroom for each twenty-five of our own young. We just have to care more about that than something else.

I have mentioned the above items only because it seems to me that they are growing symptoms of an increase in the rejection of our own young, and will make the "youth problem," which is really an adult problem worse instead of better. We can go on, of course, making our society more hostile and more rejecting of our young, but at an awful price. The price will be paid in more delinquency, more youth violence, more mental hospitals, more police, more juvenile courts.

To summarize, I hold that we adults must keep these points in mind:

1) Our culture is in jeopardy unless we can adequately care for our young.

2) Our young people are all right when we get them. If all is not well with them, it is due to what has happened to them in an adult-managed world.

3) If youth have not been too badly damaged by the life that has been thrust upon them, they enjoy and desire a good society as much as we do.

4) In urban society, our young live under more difficult circumstances than they used to.

5) The amount of juvenile delinquency in any community is a measure of that community's lack of concern for its young.

6) There is really no valid, responsible place in our urban communities for youth. They are a displaced segment of our society.

7) A place must be made for them, and it seems to me that the only feasible place is the school.

Since nearly everyone believes that the "youth problem" is getting worse as the years go by (and this certainly seems to me to be so) it would be logical to admit that we must be doing something wrong, or neglecting something we should do. Let us then try something different, something which seems dictated by the findings of researchers. Let us try:

Acceptance of all of our young as worthy, valuable, uniquely blessed with some gifts.

Making the school a real youth institution.

Involving youth in what is to be undertaken.

Choices for youth, for the development of free, creative minds.

Cooperation and democracy in the place of authoritarianism.

The human approach, rather than stressing those things which lie outside the learner.

Love, to replace alienation of so many of our own flesh and blood.

The Eyewitness Accounts of American History Series

THE AMERICAN LABOR MOVEMENT,
edited by Leon Litwack—S-44
AMERICAN SOCIALISM, 1900-1960,
edited by H. Wayne Morgan—S-85
THE CAUSES OF THE CIVIL WAR,
edited by Kenneth M. Stampp (with revisions)—S-1
THE GREAT DEPRESSION,
edited by David A. Shannon—S-10
IMMIGRATION AS A FACTOR IN AMERICAN HISTORY,
edited by Oscar Handlin—S-2
THE NEGRO SINCE EMANCIPATION,
edited by Harvey Wish—S-106
THE NEW DEAL AND THE AMERICAN PEOPLE,
edited by Frank Freidel—S-87
THE PROGRESSIVE MOVEMENT: 1900-1915,
edited by Richard Hofstadter—S-72
RECONSTRUCTION, 1865-1877,
edited by Richard N. Current—S-114
SLAVERY ATTACKED: The Abolitionist Crusade,
edited by John L. Thomas—S-109
SLAVERY DEFENDED: The Views of the Old South,
edited by Eric L. McKitrick—S-59
THE TWENTIES: Fords, Flappers and Fanatics,
edited by George E. Mowry—S-69

The Classics in History Series

The Modern Nations in Historical Perspective Series

ARGENTINA, Arthur P. Whitaker—S-601
AUSTRALIA, Russel Ward—S-610
THE BALKANS, Charles Jelavich
and Barbara Jelavich—S-611
CENTRAL AMERICA, Mario Rodríguez—S-609
CEYLON, Sinnappah Arasaratnam—S-603
CHINA, Kenneth Scott Latourette—S-607
CUBA, HAITI, & THE DOMINICAN REPUBLIC,
John E. Fagg—S-615
FRANCE, John C. Cairns—S-617
INDIA, Stanley Wolpert—S-613
INDONESIA, J. D. Legge—S-606
ITALY, Massimo Salvadori—S-612
MOROCCO, ALGERIA, TUNISIA, Richard M. Brace—S-604
NEW ZEALAND, William J. Cameron—S-608
NIGERIA AND GHANA, John E. Flint—S-618
THE PHILIPPINES, Onofre D. Corpuz—S-616
RUSSIA, Robert V. Daniels—S-602
SCANDINAVIA, John H. Wuorinen—S-614
VENEZUELA AND COLOMBIA, Harry Bernstein—S-605